CW00552559

Dear Smash Hits, We're From Scotland! :
An Alternative History of Zines & DIY Music Culture (1975-2025)

By Alastair MacDonald Jackson

Published by Earth Island Books
Pickforde Lodge
Pickforde Lane
Ticehurst
East Sussex
TN5 7BN

www.earthislandbooks.com

© Earth Island Books
First published by Earth Island Books 2024.
All rights reserved.

No part of this publication may be reproduced, distributed or transmitted by
any means, electronic, mechanical, photocopying, or otherwise, without the
prior permission of the publisher.

Paperback ISBN 9781916864283
ebook ISBN 9781916864290

Printed and bound by Solopress

Contents

Foreword

During my time in London, I visited Scotland quite a few times before, during, and after my involvement in Punk.

I love the Scottish people so much that I married a Scotsman! I have family there now, and I'm pleased that this book has been written and has a chapter on women's involvement in developing a distinctive, independent sound.

Fanzines were vital to the movement in its early days, reflecting what was happening at street level. We connected directly with the kids at our gigs; we didn't need permission from the big music labels or approval from the established music papers. We had our own fanzines!

This book acknowledges how the punk ethos reached Scotland and shows how the DIY ethic sprang up everywhere. It credits the diversity of Punk initiatives, each with its own flavour.

I had an independent spirit and developed a different style of drumming. Perhaps I influenced some girls (and boys) in this book! Having a DIY outlook and attitude is essential for every generation, and I hope that the Scottish DIY spirit that runs through this book continues to reverberate for a long time.

Paloma Romero McLardy

Cape Cod, Mass. USA. May '24

This Book is dedicated to the memory of Malky Mackenzie

Introduction

Growing up as a teenager on the Hebridean island of Skye in the 1980's, it was a common trope to hear musicians moaning about living 'in the suburbs', and by that, they usually meant a part of London no more than half an hour's train ride from the city centre. Old Janet Ballion, aka Siouxsie Sioux, was forever going on about how awful it was to grow up in Chislehurst, a grand total of 14 miles from London city centre, as if it was located in Outer Mongolia. You want to have tried living 630 miles from London, Janet. 46 miles to high school and back every day. 126 miles, and a ferry crossing, to the nearest record shop. And the nearest music venue? Goodness only knows. If you'd encountered those type of logistics, I'd have listened to your complaints as valid. Of course, at the time, you accept these 'numbers' as part of growing up, but unlike Janet, I had always wanted to live in the suburbs. They seemed really close to where the action was.

This book was spurred into action by yet another musician's moan about the suburbs, this time Tracy Thorn of Everything But The Girl, and her book 'Another Planet: A teenager in Suburbia'. Spurred by a review of how terrible it was about growing up in Hertfordshire (admittedly it does sound pretty bad), I thought it was time to counter this nonsense. I read her book, 'Bedsit Disco Queen', about how she got into playing music with Marine Girls & EBTG, and it is a well written and interesting account, but I could never fathom why living a few miles north of London would be such a handicap? So I thought it was time to set the record straight about living so far from the action, and at the same time take a look at the development of Scotland's independent music scene through the lense of its music fanzines, both of which were flourishing, but unknown to me, as I was growing up in the Hebrides. The Guardian newspaper had a music blog in 2009 which looked at the 'UK's least Rock'n'Roll Locations'. They featured the Hebridean island of Colonsay, and reading it, it could have just as easily been talking about Skye in the 1980s. Simon Reynolds in his exemplary book on post-punk, 'Rip It Up And Start Again', mentions music historians celebrating 'being in the right place at the right time', or as the case may be, in the wrong place at the wrong time.

When punk hit Britain in 1977 it had zero impact on my young life. I remember happily dancing about watching fireworks that Summer in the village Jubilee celebrations. There was no talk of Anarchy or riots in our far away lives then. Photographs of the time happily demonstrate the lack of fashion sense prevalent then on the Isle of Skye. For men, boiler suits and wellies were de-rigueur. For the ladies, a headscarf twinned with an anorak and A-line skirt. And for the young folks, flared jeans, cheap trainers and cagouls were the order of the day.

In the Autumn of 1980, I headed off to High school in Portree. Being a small town, or more accurately a large village, Portree had limited facilities in the way of vinyl or cassette offerings for eager young consumers of pop and rock. Pretty much the only items on offer were at Alastair 'Bam''s electrical emporium. A place of limited offerings indeed, where chart 7" singles had to be ordered from Inverness. When The Smiths appeared on TOTP with 'What Difference Does It Make?', I decided to make a bee-line for Mr Bam's shop. Little did I know that a 'Smiths' argument was about to ensue. For some reason, he refused to believe that there was a pop group with such a, well, family-like name. 'It's ridiculous. There's no such band... ..' For some reason he thought I was winding him up. After much backwards and forwards he was finally persuaded to take my order, and was able to look forward to the two week wait. Imagine that indie-kids of today! Portree was not the height of hipsterdom then, or ever really.

Despite being the 1980's, Skye still felt quite cut off from the mainland. Literally, as this was in the pre-bridge days, when the ferry plied its route between Kyleakin on Skye, and Kyle of Lochalsh on the mainland. We usually only made it off the island twice a year in those days, and so the mainland retained a certain mythic quality. The January gales descended annually upon us bringing inevitable power-cuts, so the house was always well stocked with paraffin lamps and candles. I have fond memories of reclining in a candlelit bath, listening to Motorhead's 'Overkill' album on a battery powered mono-cassette recorder. The simple joys of youth!

Thankfully, I also had older cousins on the mainland who shaped my musical tastes, and very kindly gave me old punk singles and let me record their albums. By the age of 14 I had a highly developed knowledge of the Clash and Damned discographies. My move into more esoteric musical territory emerged altogether more slowly. My older cousin also gifted me a leather bomber jacket with a large V on the back, which I thought was rather cool. Doc Marten boots were standard, as they could double up as school wear, going out wear, or going to the peats wear. Brilliant.............

'There was nobody older than 17. People in their 20's were ancient'! as one young turk in Skye remembers about the time when youngsters were forming school bands in the '80s. I recall being about 14 and reading that Joe Strummer had joined the Clash when he was 24. I was both shocked and appalled at that revelation. To me then, that was exactly the age you should be hanging your guitar up. Of course, when I was older I found out that many of the punk era performers were in their mid to late 20s, and people like Knox from the Vibrators was virtually picking up his pension at 31. You can see it in gig pictures of the time, when audiences look ridiculously young compared with the performers.

We had missed punk by virtue of age and geography, and the same applies

VII

pretty much to post-punk. But, around 1985 we became aware of something stirring musically in the south of Scotland. It might still have been 200 miles from Skye, but it was certainly closer, and seemed like 'ours' somehow, as if a load of bands had wrestled the reins from the London elite and rejigged punk through the lens of the 1960s. The Soup Dragons, Shop Assistants, Pastels were our generation. The new Beat Generation

Our link with the outside world of music were John Peel & Andy Kershaw on Radio one, Top of the Pops and compilation tapes made up by school mates. I'm not sure how aware we were of fanzines at the time. We'd read about them in the music papers, but whether or not we'd actually seen any before, I'm not sure. However, it was around this time that I boldly suggested to one of my school pals that he start up a zine. That was 1986, and the rest, as they say, is history.....

Chapter 1:

Bam Balam and The Rumblings of Something New

Let's reverse back even further in time now. It's February 1975. Goodness knows what I was doing? Probably kicking stones down the road on my way back from Dunvegan Primary School, dressed in shorts and scuffed wellies. I must have been in Primary 2 then. Scotland's music scene, was, quite frankly dreadful. Only Alex Harvey and his Sensational Band suggested any possibility of an alternative to porridgey pop or blues bores. A BBC Old Grey Whistle Test (OGWT) special on Scotland from that year featured hairy, heavy rock like Maggie Bell and Nazareth, the country-pop of Rab Noakes, and the long and rightly forgotten Blue. All beflared, in stack heels, and sporting straggly beards. Well, maybe not Maggie Bell. If that was the musical state of the nation, it was in a very poor state indeed.

There were however, a few folk, who, discontented with what they saw around them, decided to look back to look forward. Brian Hogg's fanzine *Bam Balam*, first appeared in February 1975 and focused on 1960s pop and psychedelia. It was cited by Mark Perry as an influence on his seminal punk zine *Sniffin' Glue*. The zine was into its fourth issue before Perry decided to start his zine in July 1976 after he went to see The Ramones at the Roundhouse in London. In Jon Savage's seminal book on punk, 'England's Dreaming', Perry insists that, 'all that stuff about Glue being the first fanzine is crap. Brian Hogg's *Bam Balam* ... showed you that you could do a magazine and you didn't have to be glossy'. His writing in *Bam Balam* was singled out by Savage who likened it to 'haiku in its simplicity and elegance'.

Bam Balam Issue 1, 1975, Scotland's First Modern Music Zine. Courtesy Brian Hogg.

Brian Hogg himself was unaware of the accolades until after the event. 'I had no idea at the time that Jon Savage and Mark Perry thought so highly of my work. I'm still touched that they did so. I met Mark a couple of times in London and I must say I always admired his take on whatever it was Punk should be. Not just with the ground-breaking *Sniffin' Glue*; his band ATV gave us one of the era's most brilliant records - 'Action Time Vision' - he unashamedly covered a song by the Mothers Of Invention and worked with both Throbbing Gristle and anarcho-hippies Here & Now. That's how it should be. Jon did reference *Bam Balam* in his Kinks biography but it wasn't until he published 'England's Dreaming' in 1991 that I was aware both would note its influence. He is a wonderful writer; I can't think of anyone else who casts such a perfect critical eye on music and culture. Greil Marcus comes close but rates too many things I can't be bothered with (post 'Astral Weeks' Van Morrison and Elvis Costello spring to mind.)'

He moved to Dunbar in 1974 to take up a teaching post, and agrees about the state of the music scene in Scotland at the time. 'Culturally it wasn't much of a wrench - live music in Edinburgh barely existed, most of the venues from the previous decade had gone and, apart from University gigs which were a pain to get into if you weren't a student, tours generally headed to Glasgow and the Apollo, as Edinburgh lacked anything remotely similar. There was the occasional exception - usually during the Fringe - but there was nothing consistent. That's why the Rezillos were so important to Scotland - they would kick open the doors enabling a whole new scene to blossom'.

'Before that point there was no real infrastructure left within Scottish music, save that encouraged by Unicorn Leisure in Glasgow. A generation of promoters, active in the 1960s, had retired. Everyone looked to London to achieve success and any sense of individuality was lost in seemed an endless succession of beige and flares. It was particularly true of the '75/76 period where hopeless band after hopeless band was declared "nice" by Bob Harris and being hirsute seemed obligatory to secure a 'Whistle Test' session. Pop acts - the Rollers, Slik - cultivated a different image but were nonetheless part of an equally established treadmill'.

'Alex Harvey stuck out because his take on pop culture and corresponding deconstructive vision - a grab-bag of Marvel Comics, Jacques Brel and greaser rock'n'roll dosed with a dash of Brecht's Epic Theatre - created something unique. That the band were shit-hot musicians as well helped immensely but his sheer presence and charisma was something else. I don't think of Alex as an influence on punk in a musical sense but certainly as a spectacle - a non-conformist with credible street credentials - he was very important. He exuded a similar 'fuck-off' attitude, disdained cliché and was also an early visitor to the Vortex (in London), checking out what was happening'.

Other writers and musician also identified Harvey's combination of strong musicianship and real or perceived violence that made them a massive concert draw in the Britain of the mid-'70s. Hugo Burnham, later of post-punkers Gang of Four later recalled the air of malevolence and violence in the air at SAHB gigs and reckons that a number of future punk musicians were watching and taking notes. Both John Lydon and Killing Joke's Paul Raven have expressed admiration for Harvey. Nick Cave covered 'The Hammer Song', and Robert Smith of the Cure enthused to Rolling Stone (Australia) in 1993, that 'People talk about Iggy Pop as the original punk, but certainly in Britain the forerunner of the punk movement was Alex Harvey. His whole stage show with the graffiti-covered brick walls – it was like very aggressive Glaswegian street theatre'.

There were other bands easing Brian Hogg through the malaise of the Mid-70s 'I loved the New York Dolls - all the brattishness of the early Rolling Stones with the same, unkempt energy and swagger. They sounded so alive in comparison with much of what was happening - or not - around them. So many contemporary albums by those I had devoured in the 1960s, whether born out of British R&B or US Acid Rock, were dull and complacent. It wasn't all gloom though - the Flamin' Groovies' 'Flamingo' and 'Teenage Head' had rarely been far from my record deck, likewise Eno's 'Here Come The Warm Jets' and 'Another Green World' and I was similarly hooked on John Cale's 'Fear', Nico's 'The End' and Todd Rundgren's 'Wizard' and 'Todd' LPs.'

Before setting up the fanzine in 1975, he had cut his rock writing in an Edinburgh publication *Hot Wacks* run by Bert Muirhead. 'It began in 1973 but I consider it a magazine rather than a fanzine as it was one several UK publications modelled on Pete Frame's *ZigZag*, all of which covered stuff from the Diaspora of US 'West Coast' music and the British 'Underground/Prog' scene. That included magazines like *Fat Angel* and *Supersnazz*. They all served a purpose but, to my mind, each lacked the zeal, single-mindedness or belligerence that made a fanzine a fanzine and not a magazine. They'd have done well at the 'Whistle Test'. Bert's taste was traditional - then-current stuff by Traffic, the Average White Band, Joe Cocker for example - which was of little interest to me. I wished to set myself apart from that whole school, and so I penned retrospective pieces while adopting a writing style heavily influenced by Sandy Pearlman and Richard Meltzer, as I was very fond of the first Blue Oyster Cult album as well. I also got to meet and interview Arthur Lee and Captain Beefheart during this period, two all-time idols, as well as Chris Darrow from (US) Kaleidoscope, a band whose first two albums I adored.'

A particular issue of Greg Shaw's *Who Put The Bomp*, dedicated to British bands of the '60s was an inspiration for him. 'When the 'British Invasion' issue of '*Who Put The Bomp*' arrived I felt liberated, here was something giving such music legitimacy in print – I wanted to do the same. Greg, of course, was a massive music fan and had a clear-cut view of what he considered to be its true path. Overall, I think my own tastes and interests are wider – the Incredible String Band, Terry Riley and Albert Ayer to thrown in three names – none of which, I'd venture, would have figured in his world view. As I said, with *Bam Balam* I wanted to focus on records and acts I considered unfairly frozen in time. It wasn't about nostalgia, it was about giving space to things I felt were being denied recognition. In many ways I felt that even more so after Punk – those with a 'year-zero' mentality annoyed me just as much the idiots who railed against the newcomers' existence.'

'I don't honestly remember how I first heard about *Bomp*. I knew of Greg Shaw's previous publication *Mojo Navigator* – I hadn't seen one then though – and had read his reviews in *Rolling Stone* etc but my instincts tell me there must have been something about him and a contact address in *Let It Rock*, a dour-but-still-worth-reading contemporary of *ZigZag*. Music traditionalists/sociologists such as Simon Frith, Dave Laing, Charlie Gillett etc were among the contributors and they would be a likely contact for Greg. All I do recall is that we sent copies of *Hot Wacks* to him in exchange for his unseen latest issue which turned out to be the above game-changer. Trading 'subscriptions' with other fanzines would later become commonplace – *The Rock Marketplace, Not Fade Away, Comstock Lode, Flashback'* etc – all hit the doorstep in similar fashion over the next few years'.

An other inspiration for Brian was Lenny Kaye's meticulously curated 'Nuggets' compilation of '60s Garage bands 'It's not that I wasn't already aware of much of its content but the fact that here was something enshrining these wonderful records was so important. What made it different from anything else in the UK was my subject matter and approach'. There was another reissue that was crucial in the tone the zine was to take. 'Charisma issued the '66/67'collection by the Creation – a band I loved – and I began thinking about other great records, lost to time, viewed as mere juvenilia, and deemed less worthwhile than the tosh many of the same bands were currently touting. I mean 'You Really Got Me' v 'Supersonic Rocket Ship'? 'My Generation' v 'The Seeker'? 'Out Of Our Heads' v 'Goat's Head Soup'? No contest in my book. When the 'British Invasion' issue of *Who Put The Bomp* arrived I felt liberated – here was something giving such music legitimacy in print – I wanted to do the same.'

He named his zine after a song by perennial underachievers The Flamin' Groovies, a band Jon Savage refers to as one of the few 'concise rock'n'roll bands in the 1970s.' 'I loved them – I'd been a fan since their debut album – and was so excited when they came over to the UK in 1972. I saw them live at the Bickershaw Festival near Manchester – yes, I was one of its sodden masses – and their singles for United Artists were superb. When it came to naming my venture it had to be after one of their songs. I initially opted for 'Yesterday's Numbers' but that seemed just too-perfect and instead chose the more cryptic *Bam Balam*'. And he has little time for the Year Zero naysayers who wrote them off after their 1976 London appearance. 'The archive recordings from the Groovies which appeared on the French-based Skydog label – 'Grease' etc – cemented a cult status akin to the MC5 but 'Shake Some Action' divided opinion on release – some were critical of its 'retro' atmosphere; those with taste and common sense saw it for the fabulous album it was.

'However, their suits and melodies were soon deemed out-of-step with bondage gear and amphetamine-charged sounds. Sharing a bill with the Ramones and (God help us) the Stranglers became emblematic of change and was seized upon by those denying anything worthwhile happening prior to 1976. I saw them again in 1978 and they were breath-taking, but by that point the backlash was in full swing and former champions had deserted in droves. I published the interview I did with them on that tour as a 'special' issue – 'Flamingo'.

All the while he was still keeping his ear to the ground for the new sounds emerging from New York. 'Television's 'Little Johnny Jewel' was a pivotal record; icy, edgy with a staggering guitar solo, it signalled the beginning of something new, aware of tradition but breaking away from it. The same was true of Patti Smith's 'Hey Joe', which I also thought superb. Along with the early Pere Ubu releases, these two singles suggested the emergence of a whole new set of possibilities and I was totally excited by it. Then the Ramones kicked it. I saw them twice and I even broke my 'big-venue' phobia and ventured into the Apollo for the only time in my life for the aforementioned, and excellent, Television. Gigs by Buzzcocks, Richard Hell, the Clash, the Damned, the Slits all followed and while in London I saw Wire who, to my mind, were the best to emerge from the UK Punk scene. 'Chairs Missing' is essential listening. I even managed to see Patti Smith while in New York in 1977 – that was amazing'.

Bam Balam enjoyed an impressive print and distribution run 'The run for each one was 1000, all of which sold out over time. There was no single method of distribution – for the first issue Jacki (my ex-wife) and I took copies down to London on the overnight bus and hawked them by banging on some doors. Rock On in Soho and Shepherds' Bush markets, Compendium Books and Bizarre Records in Praed Street were among those stocking it. The last-named was run by Larry Debay, a Frenchman with a signature green beard, who was the connection between Paris and London for the Skydog label releases'. It was probably here that several proto-punks discovered *Bam Balam* as they were among its customers.

5

'Later on Rough Trade took copies, as would Greg Shaw for the US. Once such chains were established then consignments of new issues could be sent by post. We never advertised, relying instead on an all-important 'plug' in other fanzines, the music press or even, on a couple of occasions, the John Peel Show but other than that it was word-of-mouth. It's amazing how good communication was in the pre-internet days. We eventually had a fairly big subscription list but would not go to print with a new issue until enough was in hand to pay for it, hence the erratic schedule'.

Of course, *Bam Balam* wasn't the first ever zine produced, in fact it wasn't even the first music zine. In the US, Science Fiction zines like *Wavelength, Sunshine and En Garde* had been going since the 1940s. The very first science-fiction fanzine, *The Comet*, was published in 1930 by the Science Correspondence Club in Chicago. The term "fanzine" was coined by Russ Chauvenet in the October 1940 issue of his fanzine *Detours*. *New Worlds* was a British science fiction magazine that began in 1936 as a fanzine called *Novae Terrae*. In Scotland, the sci-fi *Macabre*, which appeared in December 1939 in Edinburgh, became the first ever Scottish fanzine published. It was a carbonzine - ie. the pages are carbon-copies straight from the typewriter - the limitations of the method meant it was produced in an edition of less than half a dozen copies, few of which will have survived up to today.

Back in the US of A, several popular zines focusing on folk music culture emerged during the 1950s. Whilst these folk zines were still around in the 1960s, rock and roll zines also began to emerge. Paul Williams's zine *Crawdaddy!* was the most popular of these, launching in 1966 as a hand stapled fanzine, but it soon became popular enough to turn legit and become a full-on magazine.

As noted, Brian Hogg drew some of his inspiration for *Bam Balam* from *Who Put The Bomp* which was edited & published in L.A by Greg Shaw from 1969 onwards. Previously, Shaw had helped put together *Mojo-Navigator Rock'n'Roll News*, a mimeographed zine. Without a doubt *Bomp* was a fanzine for aficionados of such then-unfashionable future New Wave building-blocks as Surf Music, Girl Groups, Power Pop and Garage Rock. Writing for all the rock tabloids of the era, including a popular singles column in *Creem*, Shaw, in turn, gave early voice to many of rock's finest journalists, both in his first zine and then *in Who Put The Bomp*. He published great writing (notably Lester Bangs' 1971 anti-James Taylor screed) and was a tireless proselytizer for a return to youth-oriented pop, pronouncing hippies as 'the squares of the 70s', in many ways helping to shape the thinking of the next few years.

Here we go head first into the punk era. It's now Summer 1976 in the village of Dunvegan on the Island of Skye, in Scotland's Inner Hebrides. That long hot Summer which old folks recall fondly now. I'm seven years of age and helping out at the family peats. For the uninitiated, although it may look somewhat random, the cutting of the peat is highly organised. Our family had its own allotted peat bog or bank, at least 3 generations old, and we all pitched in during the Spring and Summer to get the peats cut and dried ready for taking home for the fire. Mum as usual has made flasks of tea and cheese rolls for lunch and we're all happily sitting by the side of the road, munching away, waiting for Donald Black to swing by in his lorry which we'll load up. This is a highlight of the year, as me and my brother get to sit atop the stacked crumbly fossilized lumps, rattling and bashing along three miles of single track road from the peat bog to the house. If there is a radio in the cab, which there probably isn't, it may well have been playing the current UK Number One hit song, '(I've got a) Brand New Combine Harvester' by The Wurzels. We very much identified and loved that song then, even though there were no combine harvesters in Skye. Still, with our wellies, flares and bowl cut hair we were without a doubt young Wurzels without even realising it.

Meanwhile beneath the gas-lit flares of Grangemouth Oil terminal in the south east of Scotland, a young music obsessive is writing punk rock reviews for the local paper and dreaming up plans for his own publication about faster & louder music. Whilst the rest of the country is still grooving to the strains of Boney M and the aforementioned Wurzels, he's already down in London picking up albums like the first Ramones platter. Inspired by John Holstrohm's hand written text for *Punk* magazine in New York, Lindsay Hutton knocks up a protype issue in September 1976 with speedy Essex R&B combo, Eddie the Hot Rods on the cover. '*Punk* was also a revelation because of John's handwriting and of course the whole visual swagger of it all. *Who Put The Bomp* was also something I consumed from cover to cover, as well as *Bam Balam* and *Hot Wacks*.

The first issue proper came out in April 1977, following a Damned gig at Stirling University. He took the name from the opening track of the first album by The Dictators - a proto-punk classic called 'The Dictators Go Girl Crazy!' which was released in 1975. There's a two page feature about the band inside and a rave review of the album. 'Yeah, I certainly preferred the US stuff and maintain that the Pistols, for me, couldn't touch The Dictators – or The Ramones. And yes, my interests were USA-centric because the Englishness of the Pistols bugged the fuck out of me. I always preferred The Damned'.

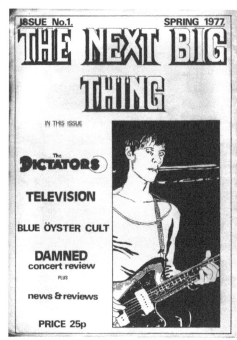

The Next Big Thing - Courtesy of Lindsay Hutton.

The Dictators could easily be described as the missing link between the New York Dolls and The Ramones, and their debut album includes a cover version of 'California Sun', a song that The Ramones subsequently covered on their 'Leave Home' album, which was released in January 1977, and also got Lindsay's seal of approval in the pages of *Next Big Thing*

'The prototype NBT had a drawing of the Hot Rods on the cover and it was printed on a die-line printer. I think *Ripped & Torn* was first by a month or something like that. NBT Issue 1 went on sale the day that The Damned played Stirling University on April 1st 1977. They did a record signing at Hot Licks in Cockburn Street, Edinburgh that afternoon. The copy of NBT that's in the National Library of Scotland was autographed by the band at the shop. The show was great. As suggested before, I rate the first two Damned singles higher than anything by The Pistols. I went on record by sending a letter stating this to *Punk* magazine that was later printed. I think it was Issue 13 with the Robert Gordon (Tuff Darts) cover. The show was a revelation'.

And what of the suggestion in some quarters that he took against Mark Perry of *Sniffin' Glue*? 'As for having a grudge against Mark, I didn't know him and might have made a few remarks but that was more to do with my being an arse than anything he did. I met him years later and found we had a lot in common. A love for Blue Öyster Cult that he kept hidden for a start. There was no grudge and *Sniffin' Glue* came up with the idea of having the staple in the corner of a pile of paper. The notion of saddle-stitch constituting what could be a magazine became a thing of the past'.

He has mixed views about the early records produced by Scottish punk outfits and he is another writer who cites the Sensational Alex Harvey Band as a big influence on punk. 'Never forget The Sensational Alex Harvey Band. That was much more punk rock than what came about. I didn't care for The Exile EP or for The Skids at the time, but that was perhaps because of a stupid prejudice that nothing really great could happen locally. That was short sighted if not stupid. The Rezillos were the exception to that rule and I'd take 'Can't Stand My Baby' over anything by The Pistols or The Clash. Maybe the Damned too. I did have the view, and still do think that Generation X were robbed'.

In 1980, he co-started The Cramps fan club — The Legion of the Cramped — along with one Stephen Patrick Morrissey prior to his becoming a Smith and rising to become whatever the sort of misanthropist he's become now. 'The Cramps first show in Europe was in Glasgow on May 31st 1979. Now that changed things for me. Mozzer and I started The Legion Of The Cramped in March 1980. He lasted three months or something and then went off to start a group of his own. My view on him now is that he gives the impression of having lost the plot. This could be a ploy but I have no interest in his oeuvre whatsoever. I never met him in real life; we were pen pals and we talked on the phone. He did invite me to see The Smiths at Night Moves in Edinburgh on their first UK tour but I declined because I thought that This Charming Man was awful and never heard from him again'. He continued with the fan club and ran its zine *Rockin' Bones* from his home in Grangemouth until the Cramps packed it in in 1983.

Rockin' Bones Courtesy Lindsay Hutton.

9

Lindsay considers himself a music fan that got lucky and that any similarity between himself and an actual journalist are, by any stretch of the most fevered imagination, entirely coincidental! 'The consideration of being thought of as a writer is still alien to me. I'm a fan that got lucky and managed to keep everything as an all-enveloping hobby. Having known people like Joey Ramone and Alan Vega to the extent that they became friends is something that absolutely baffles me but I was blessed with being around at the right time'.

Editing a zine also helped to cement lifelong friendships for Brian Hogg. 'Copies of *Bam Balam* which referenced Pere Ubu somehow found their way to a branch of Tower in Cleveland. One was picked up the group's drummer, Scott Krause who got in touch. How they got there I've no idea. The same happened in Los Angeles. Sid Griffin, later of the Long Ryders, found an issue in his local branch and he has since become a lifelong friend.'

As noted, *The Next Big Thing* was actually trumped in being the first Scottish based punk fanzine by a whisker, certainly, if you discount its prototype issue. That honour goes to *Ripped and Torn* scribed by young Tony Drayton from the new town of Cumbernauld to the north of Glasgow. 'I used to read the NME and Sounds avidly, on my commute from Cumbernauld to Glasgow. From 1973 I was buying *Disc*, but stopped getting that somewhere along the line, maybe when it merged with *Record Mirror*. I bought *Disc* as it featured the glam bands I liked at the time, Mott The Hoople, Alice Cooper, Roxy Music and of course I was a huge fan of David Bowie. Prior to *Disc* my sister used to get *Jackie* (a teeny pop magazine) and I read all the music stuff in that'.

'Moving from *Disc* to *NME* was a big step in discovering music that wasn't in the charts, and through David Bowie's mentions and support of Lou Reed and Iggy Pop, I started buying and listening to the Velvet Underground, The Stooges and from them and the *NME*, The New York Dolls. The *NME* would call these types of bands 'punk rock'.

'When in 1975 articles started appearing about a punk rock band called The Sex Pistols I was interested as they were called punk. That was the smoke signal which drew me in. As the articles got longer and there were descriptions of what this new UK punk was about, the attitude and new start, the more I knew I was part of it. How to get involved was another thing.' It became obvious with zines like *Sniffin' Glue* in London, that it was possible to just get out there and do it. 'I went to London and saw the Damned play the Hope & anchor pub in October 1976 and at the gig met Mark P. I asked him if I could write about my experience of being a Scottish punk seeing the Damned for the first time, but he didn't want me to write for *Sniffin' Glue*. Instead, he suggested that I should write my own fanzine.

'Back in Cumbernauld I thought about his words, and realised that yes, I could do this. So, with the help of my friend Skid Kid (Philip Darling), we quickly created the first issue *of Ripped & Torn'*. In Issue 2 we did a piece on The Nobodies, who were Sandy Robertson and Alex Fergusson, after we saw their advert in a record shop looking for members to form a band.' Sandy Robertson later became a writer at *Sounds* magazine, whilst Alex Fergusson joined Mark Perry in forming the band Alternative TV. From this starting point, Tony started covering the nascent, emerging punk scene in Scotland. 'In Issue 3 we published a piece edited from a long letter from singer and guitarist of The Jolt, Robert Collins, about his band. He states in it that they played their first gig on 2nd December 1976. Edwyn Collins (later to start his band Orange Juice) also wrote for *Ripped & Torn*; doing a piece in Issue 4 about the record shops in Glasgow. In that same issue I say that there's five to ten groups starting up in Glasgow and surrounding districts, then go on to say there's only one actually playing gigs, 8 Miles Out. I then write a little piece about them. This would have been written in Feb 1977. Rev Volting gets a mention in the Damned interview in Issue 4 and somewhere is a mention of him forming a band called Rev Volting And The Backstabbers. So, I was trying to find local bands to write about. At this time Edinburgh seemed like another world away'.

As Tony puts it, it was all about the music at this stage and so it's interesting to note the writers who have established themselves as experts on punk, and their intellectualization of the movement, retro fitting a raft of academic theories onto what was essentially a musical reboot of the '60s. As Danny Baker said about his time as a writer on *Sniffin' Glue*, 'we knew nuffin' about Anarchy'. Jon Savage has managed to position himself as a world expert on the subject, and let's face it, he wrote a fairly minor zine during punk, then got on board the staff of Sounds magazine. Having said that, 'England's Dreaming' is a brilliantly written book, but it does attribute an amount of post-modernist thinking onto punk, which only a few of the musicians involved would have been vaguely aware of. On the other hand, punk wasn't the working class, dole queue rock mythologised by The Clash, and later coopted by bands like Sham 69, and writers like Gary Bushell. As always, the truth probably lies somewhere in between.

Tony has his own take on this. 'Jon was in the right place at the right time, always around everywhere and anything that was happening – that was my view of him when I first met him in Rough Trade after moving to London. He loved to chat and talk; made you feel he was interested in what you were saying, but always looking over your shoulder for someone more important to talk to. Flattery gets you everywhere and Jon was one of those people born to schmooze; get a foot in the door then before you know it, he's sitting by the fire. He also achieved that by doing the heavy lifting when necessary, writing the articles and interviewing the bands without making a fuss about it. If you think England's Dreaming intellectualizes and theorizes a lot' he adds, 'then you'll hate Greil Marcus' book Lipstick Traces; which I love; seeing it as a deeper dive inside the meanings and worlds behind punk that Savage dares go into'.

'There's another figure jostling for the 'world expert on punk' title and that's Paul Gorman. His book 'The Life and Times of Malcolm McLaren' is an exhaustive look at what happened and why in the punk years, through the lens of McLaren's life and vision. If you find his blogs on the internet, Gorman has written in them many, many detailed stories about bits of punk trivia – all fascinating and well written. Gorman was at the right place at the right time being in the pub when Malcolm asked Johnny (Rotten) to come back to the shop and audition for the band'.

'The Situationism was all Malcolm and (future Clash Manager) Bernie Rhodes' idea. Jamie Reid, who went on to become the Pistols graphic designer, was also a big situationist, as was his partner Sophie Richmond (who ran the Glitterbest office for Malcolm). They had the big ideas and the debate about who wrote Anarchy In The UK still rages, but all of them had a hand in it. I think Glen wrote the tune for it. When Glen Matlock does his solo gigs he tends only to play Pretty Vacant from the Pistols era; as if this is the one he wrote, and not Anarchy. Glen working in the shop would have picked up on Malcolm's situationist ideas, because Malcolm could talk. Boy, could he talk. 'Would he ever stop', that was the question when he opened his mouth!'.

As well as continuing to produce *Bam Balam*, Brian Hogg also published a punk fanzine in 1977, enthusing about the Jam, but ultimately finding Paul Weller's voice and visuals off putting. 'I published one issue of *Away From The Numbers* in the late summer of 1977 - exactly how many I ran off don't remember - a hundred maybe? It was the product of a Gestetner rather than something professional, pinned to a photocopied cover. I really just intended it to be something to sell locally in Dunbar but a bundle went into Edinburgh shops and some sold mail-order. It wasn't a serious endeavour, I just wanted to produce something which could reflect what was happening in contemporary music but I was always determined that *Bam Balam* wouldn't become that vehicle. Its founding principle - whatever that was - would remain intact. *Bomp* embraced Punk and Power Pop/New Wave but lost its identity in the process, while *ZigZag* under Kris Needs did something similar, ejecting country-rock or such-like in favour of X-Ray Spex. That made sense, but I was never convinced by its adopting the rough & ready, sub-*Sniffin' Glue* look. It seemed a bit like dressing down for the weekend'.

That approach enabled him to retain his singular vision for *Bam Balam*, whilst at the same time tapping into the new music with a different publication. 'I was aware of the burgeoning fanzine scene in Scotland. I didn't catch on to Tony D's *Ripped & Torn* until after he moved to London, but those on my immediate radar included Johnny Waller's *Kingdom Come*, Ronnie Gurr's *Hanging Around* and Mike Scott's *Jungleland*. However, it was Lindsay Hutton's *The Next Big Thing* that interested me most. Lindsay had, and still has, a unique, unbending view with respect to good and bad in music and it's one I have the utmost respect for'.

Kingdom Come Editor Johnny Waller

'I chose *Away From The Numbers* for two reasons. I did like the Jam song of that title and was initially attracted to their Who-like style. I also thought 'In The City' was a great single. However, Weller's one-dimensional voice eventually became hard work over a whole album and my enthusiasm faltered with their Tory Party nonsense and use of the Union Jack. That had much darker connotations in 1977 than when Townsend & Co exploited a pop-art reference and it should never have been stage décor with the National Front on the march. Plus, their second LP was a stinker. The other reason for the name was because, unlike *Bam Balam*, there were no catalogue references or chart placings - it was indeed 'away from the numbers'.

*Away From The
Numbers Issue 1,
1977, Courtesy
Brian Hogg*

There was an interesting afterword involving Weller and *Bam Balam* which Brian explains. 'Weller knew of the mag & liked it and at one point he was going to publish a book by me via his Riot Stories imprint. He even mentioned it in an interview for 'The Face' in April '83. The book - titled 'Move On Up' - charted how Black music gained popularity in the UK via record releases, distribution and British bands' cover versions. I finished it but he didn't like how I approached it, thought it too dry & knocked it back'. Ironically, as an aside to the Weller tale - Simon Spence's book on the Immediate record label has been updated & republished. When 'Move On Up' was knocked back Brian suggested that as a possible subject to Paul Weller but he reckoned it much too specialised for publication. The moral of this tale is never listen to anything musicians say! Or, maybe just ex-members of The Jam...

....

There were differences between Edinburgh and Glasgow in their treatment of bands which they considered to be 'punk'. There were no issues with punk bands playing per-se, but in Glasgow, the City Fathers in their puritanical wisdom decided to 'ban' punk, but crucially only in venues which were licensed as theatres. The catalyst for this ban depends on who you listen to. Billy Sloan, a Glasgow journalist sympathetic to punk reckons that it was banned 'after a Stranglers gig at the City Halls....that's why we had to go the Bungalow Bar in Paisley'. Other sources state that the Ramones track 'Now I Wanna Sniff Some Glue' caused an apoplectic 'cooncillor' to explode, 'We've got enough glue sniffers in this city without importing them from the USA'! Sloan isn't quite correct about the Bungalow Bar though. Paisley's original 'punk pub' was the Silver Thread. The Bungalow didn't open until sometime in 1978, but he's right in that it became the most iconic, and best remembered punk venue of the era.

Whatever the case, there were still a couple of city centre pubs like the Mars Bar and the Burns Howff, where you could catch the punky stylings of a pre-Simple Minds - Johnny and the Self Abusers, or The Jolt from Wishaw. *Hanging Around* zine editor Ronnie Gurr effusively reviewed The Abusers at Glasgow Art School in late '77, '(the band) took the stage at 12.30, if indeed two orange boxes can be called a stage. The set opened with a cracking version of 'White Light White Heat. The audience of straights and wilted flower children didn't appear to enjoy it'. Incidentally, both The Jolt and The Exile from Bishopbriggs paid 'homage' to Radio Clyde DJ Tom Ferrie who actively hindered the development of punk in the city. 'Fascist DJ' was the excellently titled Exile song, and The Jolt paid 'homage' with their 'Mr Radio Man'. The Exile had released their song on their own Boring label, as part of a 4-track E.P. Entitled 'Don't Tax Me', released in August 1977, the E.P saw the band tentatively dipping their toes into a DIY/New Wave sound, and affecting odd sounding London accents. The cover showed a band in transition from a Status Quo look (double denim and 'tache), to short hair and skinny ties. Nevertheless, it was a fine self-released effort of which 1,600 copies were pressed. The band were pipped to the post in releasing an independent single north of the border by a matter of weeks by the Rezillos' 'Can't Stand My Baby', on Lenny Love's Sensible label based in Edinburgh. Love had intended for Sensible to be an important indie, but in the end only released two 7" singles.

So, with issues for the bigger touring bands, Edinburgh naturally became the place Glasgow's punks had to gravitate to. The place and time where things started to coalesce was The Clash's White Riot tour in May '77, but it was the support acts the Slits, Subway sect & Buzzcocks rather than the headliners who were the main influencers, although Lindsay Hutton plays devil's advocate on that assertion, 'The angle that it all came about after that Clash show at Edinburgh Playhouse is a premise I can't take seriously. The Hungry Beat book (about the Scottish pop underground) deals with all that if you wear that perception'. However, it's a fact that many of the protagonists interviewed for Hungry Beat testify that the Slits and Subway Sect lit the torch paper for the post-punk explosion in Scotland. It was guitarist Viv Albertine's first gig with the band and drummer Paloma Romero McLardy, known at the time as Palmolive, recalls singer Ari heading into the crowd asking for a comb. 'Yeah, I remember her doing that, and the thing about those gigs was the connection with the kids in the audience. It was all about communication, and communicating your attitude across. It was explosive'.

There were certainly some punk by numbers bands forming in Scotland like The Drive from Dundee, but pretty quickly, especially in Edinburgh, it began to take a different turn. Flowers, Dirty Reds, Fire Engines et al took an artier and more spiky swerve in the road. One of the prime movers in pushing punk forward into something more interesting was the Fast Product label set up in late '77 by Hilary Morrison and Bob Last in Edinburgh. Hilary had given Bob a copy of the Buzzcocks' 'Spiral Scratch' E.P, an ode to autonomy, and the pair latched on to the fact that it might be possible to set up a record label without any real experience. Its first release came in January 1978, with Leeds post-punkers 'Never Been in A Riot', a satirical take on the Clash's wholly fabricated outlaw-chic. A record of high intelligence, but low fidelity, it made the NME's single of the week. Fast continued to release influential early singles by the Human League and Gang of Four, before turning their attentions to local bands such as Edinburgh's Scars. They also released what they termed 'Earcoms' (ear comic compilations), the first of which featured Hilary's band Flowers, and Earcom 2 had Joy Division on it, amongst others.

Fast enjoyed playing cheeky post-modernist games before it was even a thing, witness their sheer audacity in packaging and selling orange peel in a bag, and also releasing two discursive fanzine interactions *FAST 3 – The Quality of Life and FAST 6 – SeXex*. 'Half the pleasure of a record was buying the marketing; the package', Last told me in 1996, 'therefore we would get as excited and interested in the presentation and make sure the whole thing related and made sense'. This narrative around product was quickly picked up on by the likes of Factory Records and a little later back again in Scotland by Postcard Records.

Whilst zines were crucial in the discourse around post-punk and the new music, there was little support from the national music papers or Scottish press in terms of promotion, and it was unusual for an unsigned band like Simple Minds to get reviewed in the London music 'inkies'. The Minds had received rave reviews from Scottish zines such as *The Next Big Thing* during 1978, and Ian Cranna at the NME described one of their gigs as 'a thrilling aural kaleidoscope of searing intros and instant riffs'. Lindsay Hutton explains the excitement of early Minds: 'Simple Minds was an entirely different proposition in 1978/79 as they emerged from Johnny and the Self Abusers. The Abusers certainly had a Stooges, Velvets, Roxy thing that was way more heartfelt than some of the bandwagoneers'. Edwyn Collins took great delight in dismissing the band as 'poseur neds', but Lindsay reckons that 'he tended to play to the balcony too much in retrospect, and perhaps that quip was tinged with a wee bit of jealousy?'

Following this type of exposure In December of '78 the band signed to Zoom Records in Edinburgh. Zoom was owned by Bruce Findlay who

16

owned a chain of records shops called 'Bruce's Records', which was a crucial emporium for Scotland's young punks to hang around and buy records and fanzines. In Scotland, there had been a culture of fanzines since punk that circulated round various record shops, and label and shop based zines. Guitarist James King, later of the Lone Wolves, states that Graffiti Records in Glasgow stocked *Punk* from New York and emphasises the importance of shops like Bruce's. 'People who went on to play in bands worked in record shops', like Steven Daly of Orange Juice, Brian Superstar of The Pastels & Big John Duncan (The Exploited and Goodbye Mr Mackenzie). From the shopfloor of Bruce's Records came *Cripes!*, yet another publication which Brian Hogg was involved with. It never actually claimed to be a fanzine, instead it billed itself as Bruce's Newsletter. Brian Hogg has his own views on the publication. '*Cripes!* was a promotional vehicle for Bruces - to be honest it never really pretended to be anything else with best-selling lists and back catalogue special offers. The live reviews, combined with the columns written by Bruce Findlay and myself and Xerox production, gave it something of the air of a fanzine. I find it quite amusing that it now has a cult following; I didn't even keep any copies'.

Cripes No 1 - Courtesy Brian Hogg.

'The Zoom label was, of course, featured heavily; unsurprisingly, so too were Simple Minds. I first saw them live in Edinburgh in August 1978 and the following day telephoned Bruce to suggest he do the same as I felt they would be the band to take Zoom up to a different level. He did, he agreed and, as it looked like he could be successful in signing them, I took up a long-standing invitation to go back & work with him again which I did for the best part of two years'.

'I'm not sure what I saw or heard in Simple Minds was ever captured on record' Brian Hogg still believes, 'there was a compulsive, dark mystery afoot in the early days'. Following the release of their debut album, they made two appearances on the BBC's Old Grey Whistle Test, and recorded several Radio 1 sessions. The next band from Glasgow to receive similar attention was Orange Juice, but that wasn't until 1980, and the Postcard-era. Punk was slower to mutate into what was retrospectively termed 'Post Punk' in Glasgow and there was difficulty in getting music press interest north of the border generally. Steven Daly of Orange Juice recalls, 'There was a period when I quit the band. I was pissed off with the amateurism, and during that time I worked with this Glasgow punk band, The Backstabbers.....astonishing, and if they'd come from Manchester or even Bristol, they'd have got a record deal, but no A&R man would come near Glasgow back then'. It was left to a certain Alan Horne to create that level of interest from south of the border........

Chapter 2:

A Sad Day We Left The Croft – Music Stories of the Scottish Islands

So, we've established earlier on that punk had no impact on the Highlands & Islands, or did it? How was life on the croft? My mum was a Country and Western fan in the post punk years, and there was certainly no sign of XTC or PiL in our house. Geordie Jack was the DJ on BBC Radio Highland who was the preferred radio listening choice in Dunvegan, along with Radio Nan Gaidheal (The BBC's Gaelic station). Geordie made sure that maudlin tales of lost loves and dead collie dogs by Irish and Scottish troubadours with fake Nashville accents were wafted through the airwaves on a regular basis. Unfortunately, they were also wafted into our kitchen where we always sat with the radio on. Even at a young age I knew that this wasn't a musical genre that I was going to learn to like frankly, and I still can't quite fathom out its popularity.

Hindsight coupled with the internet can be a wonderful thing. As far as I knew or cared at the time, the Highlands and Islands were a cultural desert in so far as good music was concerned, however, it turns out that the area has more interesting musical back stories than you might imagine, so read on.

The island of Lewis in the Outer Hebrides is not normally associated with the Sex Pistols, but in 1975, their future designer Jamie Reid, sold up his *Suburban Press* in Croydon, and moved north with his partner Sophie Richmond. Inspired by similarly disillusioned friends John and Carola Bell, who had recently given up their Notting Hill printing press, *Crest Press*, in order to take on a croft (the first non-islanders to do so), Reid and Richmond moved to the island and ended up staying there for a year.

Jamie Reid began writing for the Skye based newspaper, *The West Highland Free Press*, whilst he was living in Lewis. The newspaper was founded in 1972 as a left-wing weekly, but with the principal objective of providing its immediate circulation area with the service with which a local paper is expected to provide. The paper's priorities are summarised in the Gaelic slogan on its masthead: 'An Tir, an Canan 's na Daoine – The Land, the Language, the People'. It is a slogan borrowed from the Highland Land League which, in the late 19th century, fought crucial battles to win security of tenure for crofters, and would have appeared to summarize the ethos for Reid in continuing his left wing political missives that had motivated him to set up Suburban Press in the first place.

However, the reality was a little more prosaic, and he helmed 'Jim's Column' in the newspaper, which allowed him to review gigs and new music releases. In a December 1975 issue of the paper, Reid enthuses about the Bob Marley & The Wailers 'Live At The Lyceum' album, but muses that it probably isn't available at the Broadford Co-op. In a later article, he reveals that he spent a couple of months working as a roadie at Glasgow's famous Appollo Theatre, and enthuses about The Sensational Alex Harvey Band.

It was during his time on Lewis that Reid received an invitation via telegram from his old college friend Malcolm McLaren, inviting him to work on a new project. Reid had last collaborated with McLaren on his Oxford Street film from 1968 to 1971, and had last seen him in person during the set-up of McLaren and Vivienne Westwood's shop SEX in 1974. The two had kept in touch sporadically throughout this period and according to Reid, McLaren's telegram simply read: 'Got these guys, interested in working with you again'. These guys were Paul Cook, Steve Jones, John Lydon (known as Johnny Rotten) and Glen Matlock, who together were the members of a new band McLaren had named the Sex Pistols.

From then on, Reid and Richmond moved slowly towards working full-time with the Pistols. Reid moved from the Isle of Lewis to London to specifically stay in touch with McLaren, living for a while with his brother Bruce and his wife Marion, whilst Richmond went to work for the Aberdeen Free Press where she stayed until September 1976, and in fact Reid designed his first Pistols poster in Aberdeen.

The WHFP also attracted other radical writers such as Roger Hutchinson who had edited the underground magazines *Oz* and *IT* in the early 1970s, before moving to Skye in 1977. *IT* had been launched in London in 1966 at a party in London's Roundhouse featuring music by the Soft Machine and Pink Floyd. *Oz* followed in 1967 and was a chaotic mess, redeemed by its use of innovative designers like Barney Bubbles, who became famous for designing record sleeves for Hawkwind, The Damned, Elvis Costello and Ian Dury, and Martin Sharp who wrote the lyrics to the Cream song, 'Tales Of Brave Ulysses'.

Roger had cut his teeth on *Styng,* which he describes as 'a sort of *IT* of the north of England. We were ahead of the curve on music. Dylan, The Stones, Beatles, Jefferson Airplane'. After making contacts via *Styng,* Roger ended up working with and socialising with some of the best music writers like Nick Kent, Mick Farren and Charles Shaar Murray. Many of these writers got poached by the mainstream music press, and allied with a lack of revenue, it started to spell the death of the underground press in the mid 1970s. When Roger visited the WHFP office in 1976, he was surprised to find they had their own print machine. 'Printing costs had done in the underground press. The paper was self sufficient in a way we could only have dreamed of'.

Interestingly, one of the founders of the WHFP, Jim Innes, had wanted the paper to follow in the tradition of the underground press, but was reined in by one of his co-founders, Brian Wilson (no, not that one!). Quite sensibly, as I'm not sure mid-70s, Gaelic speaking Skye was ready for rants and diatribes from Mick Farren and Nick Kent acolytes.

The nearest the islands got to having an underground press was when the *Free-Winged Eagle* landed on the shelves of Orkney newsagents in the Spring of 1979 – or, at least, on three of them. Others refused to stock it. The front cover of the inaugural issue proclaimed that the magazine was for 'the only cull worth having – for an autonomous Orkney, based on self-managed collectivism, individual freedom, solidarity and fun!' It was perhaps the only anarchist magazine to have been produced in the Scottish Islands. The style mixes punk and academic analysis, political rhetoric and speculative theology, with plenty of humour. The back page of the first edition includes reviews of the Orkney West Mainland Goat Society Journal ('very informative') and the Kirkwallian ('very progressive by school standards').

Free Winged Eagle – Courtesy Josie Giles

Musically, If London was burning in 1977, the Highlands were maybe smouldering slightly. The cover of Runrig's 1978 'Play Gaelic' album shows the band resplendent in flares and tank tops, like it was still 1974. But there were a few bands on the Eastern and Northern coasts of the Highlands like The Tools, The Hormones, Radio City, and The Cut that were taking a more punky direction, and the first great vinyl outing from the far north came in 1980 with Inverness-based These Intrinsic Intellectuals 'Radio Iceland' – a post-punk exercise in absurdity.

do the executive !!

EXECUTIVE

ICELAND
ICELAND

RADIO
RADIO
RADIO

RORY BLACK : TEXT.
GREGOR MORGAN : BASE.
NJAL MACDONALD : GITARR.
JOHN GODSMAN : TRUMMOR.

*Those Intrinsic
Intellectuals –
designer
unknown*

The single was enthusiastically reviewed in the September 1980 issue of *Smash Hits* '..sounds like the Undertones meet Devo. Two busily, but energetic songs, with extremely catchy tunes...very cleverly packaged in its own plastic bag'. You can almost see the reviewer getting their AA road map of the British Isles out and scratching their head over mention of Skye and Uist.

Ian Cranna in *The Face* that year interviewed main man Rory Black,who was originally from Waternish on Skye. Rory who formed the band in Inverness with other island emigres from Uist whilst he was at the time working in DR Records in the town. The single was recorded on Croft Studio's 4-track in a converted garage in Lewis, which cost the band £100 in ferry fares alone. Rory tells Cranna that they are really folk musicians, but use electric guitars 'because there's some good folk musicians, but people won't listen to it because they're into Killing Joke. So, you electrify it and it works well' Was he being entirely serious – we'll probably never know.

Also released a year later in 1981 was the 'Sad Day We Left the Croft Compilation', recorded on the island of Lewis by various local punkily inclined youth such as The Bland, The Rong, The Subjects, Bruce Wayne Band, Noise Annoys, Battery Boys and Dirty Girls. The album was recorded at the aforementioned Croft Studio at Tong, about 5 miles from Stornoway, and was first released in 1981 as a 12-inch vinyl LP on an independent record label, Adult Entertainments, based in Stornoway, and also on a cassette version by Croft Recordings.

No, It's Not The Undertones! The Rong from the Isle of Lewis (1981) Courtesy Iain Morrison.

Punk legend Johnny Moped reckons that this is 'one of the best punk compilations from that era', but 'one band stops this from being an all time classic – Addo. A bunch of Dire Straits wannabes. You know their Dads' owned the studio, or paid for the LP?'. Actually, it was the guitarist's cousin, Calum Iain, who was putting it together, and they needed two extra tracks. So, that was them on the LP then.

Drummer from The Rong, Iain Morrison recalls sprinting up to his granny's house to watched Top of The Pops on her black and white television. That was in 1977, and the event was the Sex Pistols playing 'Pretty Vacant'. 'That was my first experience of punk. We formed the band late 1978, and it was pretty standard punk. We were big Ramones fans, and their songs were easy to learn. The only people we upset were a group of Elvis fans on the island. They hated us! At dances in Stornoway, everybody was shouting for Lynyrd Skynyrd's 'Freebird'. There was absolutely no way we could play that, even if we'd wanted to'.

He's not sure how that idea to put together an album came about, but it was financed by guitarist for the Gaelic folk group Na h-Òganaich, Noel Eadie, who'd recently moved back to the island and set up the recording studio. He agreed to do it for nothing, and release 1,000 copies on vinyl, under the agreement that he could also produce and sell a cassette version himself. Of course, this seemed like an excellent idea to young Iain who'd just turned Seventeen. 'We started writing our own songs, and a couple of the older guys got bands together. I remember going down to Edinburgh to get test pressings, and Fast Product helped us out. It was great, but I'm not sure what happened to the recording copyright!'

23

Noise Annoys and Battery Boys also released a split single which was played on the Peel show on Radio 1, where he talked about being in the mood to move 'somewhere windswept that evening'. Additionally, Noise Annoys were compiled, along with Those Intrinsic Intellectuals, on 'Kilt By Death : The Sound of Old Scotland', a semi-official CD-R put together by Michael Train, an American fan of Scottish alternative music, in 2005. The Rong's track from the 'Croft' album was also compiled by Michael for the Kilt By Death 4 cassette in 2016, along with the band Dirty Girls who also appeared on 'Croft'.

At the same time, and worth a mention, were the self-appointed arbiters of Avante Gaelic Obscurist Folk Rock (AGOFR), The Guireans. According to their website the movement 'exhibited a wide variety of styles and influences, the only obvious common threads being their complete musical ineptitude and the myopic scope of their lyrical subject matter.' The Guireans shared little with the majority of AGOFR bands other than the fact that they too were 'crap and sang about tractors, peats, sheep, fish and Cathy Dhall's'. If you are in any way au fait with Hebridean culture, it's a hilarious deep dive into a world of bothies, boiler suits, woodbine roll-ups and the aforementioned tractors etc. I wonder if modern day 'Leodhasaich' (natives of Lewis) troubadours, Peat & Diesel, were in their cots listening? Anyway, as they themselves state, the Guireans have gone on to 'perpetrate a catalogue of cassette atrocities that has spanned four decades'.

Also with a Lewis connection were The Cateran, who formed in Edinburgh in the mid-1980s, with a line-up comprising of Inverness natives Sandy Macpherson and Cameron Fraser, Murdo MacLeod from Lewis, Kai Davidson, born in Shetland, and Andy Milne. Davidson had played with Inverness' first punk band, The Hormones & several bands in the early 1980s, including Reasons For Emotion, which also featured Craig and Charlie Reid, later finding fame as The Proclaimers. They were initially influenced by US acts such as Hüsker Dü and the Dead Kennedys, and signed to the DDT label. Highlights included the band playing with Grant Hart on his first UK appearances after the demise of Hüsker Dü the first shows Nirvana ever played outside of North America came sandwiched between headliners Tad and The Cateran.

The final Lewis connection comes courtesy of the indie band, Astrid. Three of the band, Charlie Clark, Willie Campbell, and Gareth Russell were born on the island, and although they had differing record collections they found a shared interest in '60s pop music. They formed the band in Glasgow, had their debut album produced by Edwyn Collins, following which, Gareth Russell went on to play bass for indie stalwarts, Idlewild.

....

Scots born elfin folk star and psychedelic poet Donovan was famous for a string of well-received record releases in the 1960's, including Mellow Yellow, Catch the Wind and Universal Soldier. Less widely known was his sojourn at Stein, on Skye's Waternish peninsula, where he, his manager Gypsy Dave Smith (who I saw in the '90s supporting Julian Cope at the Findhorn Foundation – strange karma) and a group of followers formed a commune, as only 1960s hippies could do.

I've been able to glean almost no facts about the Skye commune (but let's face it, isn't amnesia an inevitable part of the commune experience?) Those who made contact recall the episode with mild amusement. Apparently, he bought three offshore islands & three houses in 1972, as rich hippies did. I recall poking round the place (must have been the boathouse) with my parents years later after it had been abandoned, and we all commented how huge the bath was! No doubt some interesting goings on there..........

Skye's neighbouring island of Raasay has some odd musical connections as well. The township of Eyre in Raasay's southeast was home to the composer Harrison Birtwistle from 1975 to 1983. His experience of the island left an 'indelible imprint' on his string-quartet piece The Tree of Strings, its title taken from a poem by Raasay born Sorley MacLean, and Duets for Storab, which evokes a Viking-era legend. The matchmaker in getting Birtwistle to the island had been Birtwistle's friend, the sonic visionary and former geologist Peter Zinovieff, selling Birtwistle a house at Eyre and then revisiting often with family in tow. Zinovieff's EMS company made the VCS3 synthesizer in the late 1960s. The synthesizer was used by many early progressive rock bands such as Pink Floyd and White Noise, and Krautrock groups, as well as more pop-oriented artists, including Todd Rundgren and David Bowie, and my personal fave, Brian Eno. I spoke to his daughter Sofka a few years back and she recalls with great fondness, family holidays on the island during the Summer. 'Jon Lord of Deep Purple described dad as a mad professor type:' He said 'I was ushered into his workshop and he was in there talking to a computer, trying to get it to answer back!"

On a more punkish note, and now more widely known, is the fact that Joe Strummer's grandmother was born in the crofting township of Umachan in the wild north end of Raasay. I think had we known this as teenagers it might have changed our view on cultural deserts. Skye writer DJ MacLennan takes up the story from a local perspective. 'Yeah, my auntie Chrissie died, and there was a piece about her in the WHFP. It mentioned that she had been related in some way to Joe Strummer, and my Mum was saying that she used to talk about this complete tearaway in the family! So,

25

my mum worked out that Joe's granny and my granny were sisters, so that makes me his second cousin once removed. I don't think he ever made it to Raasay, but he intended to. When my pal, who is a music writer found out about this, he said we needed to go to this really remote spot at Umachan, where Clash bass player Paul Simonon had already visited. My partner Sarah and I went over and scouted the place, and found the ruin of the house where the two sisters had lived. So, we then organized a trip with friends and my brothers and went over on a very wet day, which is amazing. Back in school we couldn't see any connection between that world and ours, so to have known that then would have been quite life changing. I mean, if we'd known at the time, there was probably a chance that we could have got Strummer up to Skye'.

Regarding that wet, wild trip made to Raasay by Simonon, writer Chris Salewicz and Glasgow based journalist Damien Love also trudged through the moors with him. I spoke to Damien about the trip and mentioned fact that Clash are so often associated with the Westway in London. 'I know what you mean – I guess with The Clash you think of London first, but the international thing comes close behind. Both their music and their outlook developed into something more global pretty quickly as the band went on. And, of course, with Strummer, that citizen of the world thing was there from the very first – he was born in Turkey, after all, and had Armenian and German ancestors on his father's side. I was aware he had a Scottish side of the family through his mother, but I didn't really know much about it and, yeah: walking deeper into the more silent, barren stretches of Raasay felt a long, long way removed from any kind of a rock and roll thing. It felt quite removed from everything.

'However, the whole trip took on a stranger and much more personal feel – it was something about Joe Strummer the man rather than 'Strummer' the image/ icon, or even the musician, largely because of Paul Simonon, who did really seem to be thinking about Joe a lot during the days of that expedition'. But his Scottish heritage started creeping into his work towards the end of his life didn't it? 'Well, Strummer's stuff increasingly took on the dimensions of what we used to call "world music," with a really wide range of influences in the stew, from jazz to hip-hop to folk roots to desert music and on and on. He started out under the influence of Woody Guthrie, and later played with The Pogues – so he was undoubtedly aware of folk songbooks and a lot of traditional Scottish and Irish tunes, ballads, etc'.

'He spent some time visiting family in Scotland and Glasgow growing up, and those kinds of get-togethers can sometimes involve a song or two coming out as the night wears on – the kind of campfire mood he always tried to bring to gatherings, from what I've heard. His writing makes references to lots of things. (I always remember him quoting "I belong to

Glasgow" in his notes for Pennie Smith's book of Clash photographs - I think it was in there.) Rather than curating and preserving traditional songs in aspic and protecting them from any outside infection or change (although this is also vital, of course), the truly valuable, and living, "folk tradition" is the mongrel tradition, taking stuff from everywhere and customising pre-existing songs into something else (taking old tunes and putting new words to them, etc, exactly the way jazz, blues and hip-hop have always done) and I think his music has a lot of that spirit in it'.

I wondered if Damien had got any sense of the man himself on that wet pilgrimage across the moors . 'A bit, I think, but not so much from being there on Raasay specifically, as from listening to Paul talk about him. I was there specifically to ask him about Joe, of course. And he wouldn't have been there making that trip without Joe. And I guess the particular atmosphere of the place – the silence and space, the feeling of being far away from everything, and the lack of distractions – focussed his thoughts in a different way than if we'd been doing it anywhere else'.

'Paul spoke of Joe very much as an elder brother, someone who had helped teach him ways of thinking and looking and being. When I asked him to sum up Joe, he said "passion really" – meaning passion just for being alive, taking it all in, whatever it was, whether it was sharing a bottle and talking or travelling to play a gig. Simonon summed up the philosophy he'd learned from Strummer to me along the lines of: 'Either you're Robin Hood or you're Stalin, and the choice is really quite clear."

Had been some plan to get three quarters of The Clash back together, or if it was something which Simonon himself had wanted to do? 'The trip was originally the notion of a commissioning editor at the Sunday Herald newspaper – but the original idea was a little different. I think they'd heard about the Future Forests/ Rebel's Wood project on Skye, and then came up with the idea of asking Paul to go there – to Skye - to paint the forest site. You have to remember that Paul had really very much stopped doing music all together at this point (years later, he started playing again as a core member of The Good The Bad And The Queen, and it was brilliant to see him onstage with the bass again). He was concentrating solely on his painting, so this was a great little idea, and all really built around his work as an artist'.

'The idea of contacting Mick or Topper for the trip didn't come up – it was all about asking Paul to paint Rebel's Wood. The paper asked me to go along and document the project and do the story because I wrote for them regularly, and because they knew I was a Clash fan. I had never had any contact with Paul before that. But he's an incredibly friendly guy, I found, and it was very quickly like talking to someone you had known for ages. I interviewed Mick once, and had tried to get Joe to talk a couple of times during the 1990s - what they call "wilderness years" – when he wasn't making much new music, but he didn't want to do an interview at that point'.

'But then - it was Paul himself who came up with the idea of going to Raasay to find the ruins of the cottage, an idea inspired by his meeting with Joe's cousin, and memories of Joe roughly talking about the Scottish side and wanting to make a trip there. And that idea of Paul's changed the entire nature of the trip and the project, and made it far more meaningful, I think. He was making the trip "for" Joe, and both his absence and his presence were kind of floating around in the quite places.' Simonon must have been in Inverness when they played the Ice Rink in 1985, and he had been on a camping trip to Skye with his dad before, but perhaps the northern wastes of Raasay, were still a a shock to the system? 'The rain was pretty crazy at some points, but I don't think it was anything he wasn't prepared for. He'd travelled far and wide, and he had spent a lot of his time doing landscape paintings outside in all kinds of places and weathers. I got the impression that he just took it as it came, and acted accordingly'.

It was, by all accounts, a chilled out vibe, despite the atrocious weather. 'Aside from talking about the project and Paul and Joe, it was just general chit chat – he was asking about Glasgow, because he had memories of it from The Clash days. During the walk out to the cottage, a lot of the talk was about trying to remember where it was. I was asking him about himself a lot for the piece that I was going to write, and he had some pretty funny stories about playing a session with Bob Dylan. But, yeah, off the meter, we were just chatting. I remember he had some good things to say about the food at Raasay House, as well'.

Around the time the classic Clash line up was fragmenting in 1983, there was a strange visitation in Skye when Echo and The Bunnymen kicked off their Highlands and Islands tour at the Skye Gathering Hall in Portree in August 1983. It's hard to fathom just how bizarre this seemed at the time when the only bands to have graced the boards were folk or ceilidh bands. We had one heavy metal band from Fort William playing a dance in the Dunvegan hall, but I mean, The Bunnymen! That was a whole lot different. Manager Bill Drummond, that well known psychogeographic prankster, had cooked up the idea from some folksy, psychedelic dream no doubt . 'The notion of playing in the Hebrides grew out of various conversations we'd been having. I'm Scottish anyway, and I'd been to the islands when I was a teenager, and I was particularly impressed by the circle of standing stones at Callanish on Lewis. It seemed like a romantic thing to do'.

Ah, Bill Drummond, the man who went to the island of Jura with his KLF bandmate Jimmy Cauty to burn a million 'quid'. Allegedly. Well, I've slept out on the moors of Jura with the swirling mist and the eerie lowing of stags. It's a mystical place where strange things may or not happen. Certainly, Drummond was attuned to psychic vibrations, cosmic parabola and topographic oddities. 'Bill had this big thing for standing stones and ley lines, a lot of our tours were set along those lines, this was Bill's way of planning', Les Pattinson, the Bunnymen's bass player tells me. But it seems that the band were relaxed about Drummond checking Ordnance Survey maps for ancient tumuli, rather than the more conventional approach. 'To be honest, we hated the touring circuit in the UK, it was so honed to an old rock and rock standard, so when Bill mentioned a tour of the Hebrides we were in. It was right up the Bunnymen's street!'

My school mate Colin Wilson also recalls the event, 'Bands never came to Skye, so it felt like a dream when we heard that the Bunnymen were coming to Portree. For two nights before the gig, the pubs were heaving with goths and Siouxsie lookalikes, like an invasion'. Journalist Max Bell covering the gig for The Times newspaper gushed 'The Gathering Hall, Portree, has resounded to many a meeting of the clans in the last 100 years but it can seldom have witnessed such a fervour as on the night that Echo and the Bunnymen played there. Playing in weird settings always brought out the best in them. The Gathering Hall was a lovely old building with a wooden balcony, and it had an almost school-like atmosphere'.

And Les Pattinson confirms that a very relaxed atmosphere pervaded the whole journey. 'It was such an adventure getting there, sharing the trip with Bunnymen fans and press on the ferry, all very respectable and coolness was kept. I remember buying a fishing rod in Portree it was that kinda relaxing tour, to be honest we felt no pressure and fans wanted to have a great time, it was such a great atmosphere'.

Colin Wilson again, 'We'd only ever been to ceilidhs in the hall, and I was literally pinching myself to make sure that it was actually happening as I walked down the road. It was brilliant and the band were on fire. The place was so packed that sweat was dripping off the roof onto us. 'Never Stop', with the big glockenspiel was the song that stood out as being really amazing'. Les agrees. 'The songs worked just as well in the Gathering Hall as they did at large festivals, which was a good measure for us'. And as for Bill Drummond? Well, he behaved himself, apparently.

It certainly sounded like a great night. And I conspired somehow to completely miss it! With the passage of time, I don't really know how or why. My parents wouldn't have been happy, and as I was still only 14 at the time, and a part-time rebel, so I probably huffily agree not to go, just to keep the peace. Maybe I should have just sneaked out anyway.................

There was however to be no such disaster when the Psychedelic Furs announced that they were also coming to Portree the following year.

Maybe this was the start of every great band touring the islands? I duly went into MacIntyre's, the newsagents, and ordered my tickets, only for the band to cancel a few weeks later. Lack of sales or something like that. And that was it until 1989, when goth rockers, The Mission did a Highlands & Islands tour which took in Dingwall, Aviemore, Stornoway & Portree. Guitarist Simon Hinkler remembers the experience fondly. 'It was a magical experience. The weather was bright and the air was bracing. Of course I had The Skye Boat Song in my head, as I'm sure many thousands of people had done before. Crossing to an island gives you a sense of going somewhere special; unlike the ordinary world on the mainland, and that was certainly my experience that first time...and since'.

'We did this package deal through the fan club for the whole Highlands and Islands tour, and exactly 101 people signed up for it. Naturally, we dubbed them 'The Dalmatians'. It turned out to be a wonderful shared experience for all of us. Many of them were on the same ferries, staying in the same hotels... we'd see them in the pubs and in the street. The whole lot of us were having a special time that I'm sure none of us will that ever forget. I've often said, of all the tours in all the countries over all the years, that Scottish tour stands out as my favourite thing I ever did in this band'.

And on playing the Gathering Hall, 'it was probably the most quaint place I've ever played. For 48 hours Portree was overrun with our lot and the locals didn't know what hit them. I remember there being high jinks in the hotel corridor and a band member, who shall remain nameless, set a fire extinguisher off in the early morning. Next morning the landlady made him clean it up, and he had with a horrific hangover!' By this point in time I'd left school, and was at living in Glasgow, so seeing bands was no longer an impossible dream. It was nice however, to be back for the Summer to hear 'Wasteland' wafting through the dry ice where the accordians once played.

There was also a bit of local post-punk action with youngsters, The Thing Upstairs, featuring the above-mentioned DJ MacLennan, who recorded a one-off video 'Nan Soluis Dhubh' a sprightly cajun-punk track, for a BBC Gaelic 'yoof' show Brag in 1988. This track later resurfaced on the 'Gaidhlig Na Laisair' compilation album on Problem Records. Interestingly, as DJ himself says, 'we had never as a band, written or played any form of Gaelic music, but there was no question of our resisting the lure of publicity or BBC fees'

In more recent years local boy Mylo (Myles MacLennan) from Broadford in Skye hit the charts when the single "Doctor Pressure", a mash-up of his own song "Drop the Pressure" and Miami Sound Machine's "Dr. Beat", peaked at No. 3 on the UK Singles Chart in 2004. And since those heady

30

days of the Eighties, the island has seen Primal Scream, Calvin Harris and The Buzzcocks playing the Skye Festival with Hot Chip & Andrew Weatherall playing DJ sets in Portree. Who'd have thought it?

The islands in general have seen musicians and record label owners setting there. Ex-Idlewild frontman Roddy Woomble now calls Mull home. Buzzcocks drummer John Maher settled in Harris about twenty years ago, and now makes a living there as a photographer, and is involved with community activism. The inner Hebridean island of Eigg is home to Lost Map Records run by Johnny Lynch, who moved to the island in 2013 with his partner, a native of the island. I caught up with Johnny when I was up visiting, but my mate Mark, who I was staying with, had warned me that Johnny would probably forget that we were coming round. As we headed down the track to Johnny's house, perched stunningly on a headland by the sea, we picked our way through bikes, training shoes & wellies casually discarded around the place. Johnny spotted us through his window, and threw the door open, 'Sorry, I forgot totally that you guys were coming!'...
.........He's a genuinely friendly soul though, and pretty soon mugs of tea were brewed, and we headed up to the bothy which he rents out for tourists in the Summer, and which doubles up as a practice pad and recording studio out of season.

Johnny has always been a fan, and a practitioner of the DIY ethos in music. Growing up, his favourite band was The Beta Band, who originated in Fife. 'I think I possibly read about them, in those monthly music mags, before actually hearing them. Such a glorious collage of sound. They used to release a zine with their music - *Flower Press* - which, like their music, was a cut'n'paste mish-mash of images, drawings, doodles, photos, and writing. What I loved about The Beta Band was that they opened an entire world of art - not just their recorded music, but their inventive videos, *Flower Press* zines, their unique live show and DJ mixes. It was an education for me'.

As has Eigg, by all accounts. Johnny was previously part of Fence Records, the independent record label and musicians' collective based in the East Neuk of Fife that launched the careers of musicians such as KT Tunstall, King Creosote and James Yorkston. 'Eigg is a special place. It feels totally removed from reality, and there's a sense of absolute freedom, here. For me, it was the perfect place to launch Lost Map - as it took all of the pre-conceptions of what a label should be away, allowing me to experiment more. When I was living in Fife, I was part of a loose-knit collective of singer-songwriters, who were recording themselves at home, primarily. It was fine, but a lot of the music we released all sounded very similar. I'm the only person on Lost Map that lives on Eigg, and so the label has been more about a sense of discovery from everywhere outside of here. That sense of discovery is really what the thrill of music is all about, for me'.

When Johnny left Fence, most of the roster came with him to Lost Map, and he has an impressive and eclectic spread of musicians on the label, and involves himself in a wide range of activities which allow him to put the island and the music front and foremost. 'I put on a semi-regular festival here, called Howlin' Fling! - as well as run a sporadic residency series called VISITATIONS. Both of these projects allow me to invite artists to the island, and I've found that really rewarding. Folks love travelling here'

Image of Johnny Lynch courtesy Alastair MacDonald Jackson.

Chapter 3 :

Aftershock –Fanzines and the Fallout of Punk

Following the lead of pioneering zines like *Bam Balam, Next Big Thing* and *Ripped & Torn* in in Scotland, an explosion of zines emerged that were as important as John Peel or the music press for finding out about new music and what other people thought of it. The punk subculture was either ignored, exploited or misinterpreted by the mainstream media, and punk zines began to document the scene, on a DIY basis, making punk one of the most self-documented subcultures in history. Punk fanzines were produced simply and cheaply and distributed at gigs, meetings or by mail order. In a pre-internet age, they served an important purpose in serve as a means of connecting local scenes within Scotland to national UK scenes and international scenes, such as the US underground.

Inspired by the likes of the Desperate Bicycles and Scritti Politti's records, zine writers often encouraged their readers to create zines of their own, even to the extent of writing 'how to' guides which would generally include a breakdown of how much everything cost. The Deperate Bicycles had recorded their first single for the princely sum of £153. Their second single ends with the strident DIY rallying cry 'it was easy, it was cheap – go and do it!' The singles were self-released on their own Refill label, and distributed by hawking them around record shops in much the same way as fanzine editors did. Scritti Politti's '4-Sides' released in 1979 builds on the Bicycles DIY themes and lists all the prerequisites for releasing a record – recording, mastering, pressing, printing labels, and their associated costs.

In line with these themes of autonomy and self-determination, moving into the post-punk period, many of the anarcho-zines increasingly became vehicles for non-musical content. The band Crass, who released their E.P 'The Feeding Of The Five Thousand' in 1978 were independent, self-determinist and espoused the personal politics of anarchy. Tony D, reviewing the record in *Ripped & Torn* states that 'this record is an assault on all the phonies and liggers who've built up around the original concept of punk, free-loading and sucking vital energy away into their own pockets'. The band actively engaged with zines and were proactive in granting reviewers access for interviews. Crass were important in reintroducing 'peace' as a concept in their music, one which the more nihilistic Sex Pistols would no doubt have dismissed as a hippy hangover from the 1960s.

Many of the early 80s zines in Scotland, encouraged by the themes emerging on Crass' and other anarcho-bands' records, began introducing content which offered alternatives to that perpetrated in the mainstream media. The production of fanzines, flyers and leaflets was absolutely crucial to the growth of the movement. *Last Hints*, edited by The Clydeside Anarchists from Glasgow, had a front cover illustration based on Edvard Munch's 'The Scream', and this theme is reflected throughout the zine. Tommy Kay, a member of the Anarchist group, and a printer by trade, was instrumental in setting up the Groucho Marxist record label in nearby Paisley. In setting up a branch of Rock Against Racism in the town, he brought politics to the label, which released four 7" singles between 1979 and 1981, and paints a vivid portrait of one of the most vibrant post-punk scenes in the country.

Last Hints – Edited by Clydeside Anarchists.

Guilty of What was an anarcho zine from Stirling edited by youngster Chris Low, who was still at school, and featured articles on the standard, anarcho-punk topics: nuclear disarmament, apartheid, and fox-hunting, and featured bands like Crass, Flux, Discharge, Anti-Pasti and The Fakes from Stirling. The zine was photocopied at work by his dad. He was also the drummer for an early line up of the anarcho-punk band, Political Asylum, which was comprised of school friends from Stirling High School. *Death On A Summer's Day*, a Fife based zine was similarly based, but by that point, the editor had taken a strong anti-war and anti-nuclear stance, and was actively involved in protest marches.

Other zines began to document the emerging independent pop scene in Scotland, focussing on labels like Postcard Records, with its roster of Orange Juice, Aztec Camera and Josef K. There were standard punk zines still around, and there was plenty of space for in record shop racks for an eclectic range of publications.

Douglas MacIntyre of early '80's band Article 58, who later went on to set up the influential Creeping Bent record label, enthuses about the fanzines coming out of Scotland at the time, 'I was an avid fanzine reader when I was a teenager in the early 80s, which I would buy on trips to Impulse in East Kilbride. If I had enough money I'd get the bus and train to Glasgow and buy fanzines and a single at Blogs or similar record shops. My favourite fanzine was *Ten Commandments*, which featured great writing by Kirsty McNeil and Robert Hodgens, and photographs by Robert Sharp. The edition with Orange Juice on the cover around the time of Blue Boy being released on Postcard was a game changer, and resulted in McNeil and Sharp being picked up by the NME to work for them. Hodgens became Bluebell, and along with Aztec Camera and Jazzateers, The Bluebells became part of the second wave of Scottish independent pop. The Pastels' fanzine, *Juniper Beri-Beri*, was also really good'.

Hodgens/Bluebell was certainly in the right place at right time. He was hanging about at Postcard HQ, a shabby flat in Glasgow's west end, and got to know the characters on the scene. He recalled to *Quake* magazine in 1984 that he had 'made up imaginary groups' in the zine, 'cause there weren't many groups going. Well, this other fanzine called me up and said they'd like to hear some of these groups, so I said I'd get a hold of them. So, I went home and recorded this song and it ended up on their tape. Then a few weeks later Alan Horne (of Postcard), phoned me up and said he had to hear this track. When he found out it was me, he suggested I start a group up'. That particular phantom band recalls Bobby was '007, which led to me writing my first song 'She Hates Travel' and further to Horne's suggestion directly led him to forming his first band.

His bandmate in The Bluebells, Ken McCluskey, remembers him as an eager participant on the scene. 'My brother David and myself met Bobby when he interviewed us for his *Ten Commandments* fanzine. We were playing with our mates Dixie Deans and Donald Kerr in our school punk band Raw Deal at The Mars Bar on Howard St, supporting Altered Images and Bobby was very keen on us at the time. 'Fanzines were very popular, and the many record shops like, Listen, Bloggs, Echo, Bruces etc sold a great variety of them from *Ten Commandments* to *Sniffin' Glue*, *Stand and Deliver*, *Honey at The Core* and *Catch Crabs At The Seaside* amongst a plethora of others. We read everything'.

As the punk had morphed through to post-punk, and the new pop era was ushered in by record labels like Fast Product in Edinburgh and Postcard in Glasgow, fanzine editors began to grapple with where music was going next. *Born Yesterday*, from 1981, throws the reader a breadcrumb trail following the trajectory from punk to post punk, through to the next wave of Scottish pop: '1977 – The Ramones, 1978 – the Buzzcocks, 1979 – the Undertones... and this year it took a while but I finally fell for... Orange Juice!'. That last named band were of course the flagship band for Glasgow's Postcard record label, which became the self-styled, and not entirely tongue-in-cheek 'Sound of Young Scotland'. What all these bands had in common was a direct lineage back to the 1960s – The Beach Boys, Velvet Underground, Shangri-las and The Byrds. Unbeknown to most zine editors, labels like Creation were about to foist a ton of bands even more directly influenced by that decade on an unsuspecting public. The Jesus & Mary Chain, Biff Bang Pow!, Revolving Paint Dream et al would lead to the start of the fetishization which would leak into the mainstream charts via bands like REM and The Bangles.

Stefan Kassell from Marina Records in Germany was, and is a massive fan of the Postcard bands. He recalls hearing Orange Juice's 'Blueboy' on BFBS radio for the first time. 'The track really spoke to me. New, different music. Ramshackle, heartfelt and totally brilliant! I also heard Aztec Camera's 'Pillar to Post' on there for the first time. It totally thrilled me. Goosebumps all over'.

Postcards Records Zine - Editor Barb, copyright Postcard Records.

Much has been written about the Postcard label, not least in Simon Goddard's excellent book 'Simply Thrilled', but there were other important labels around in Scotland which have been overshadowed by the media's focus on Postcard. Adrian Thrills notes in a 1980 issue of the NME that Postcard are 'only the tip of the iceberg....an ocean which engulf bands as diverse as FK9, The Cuban Heels, TV21 and The Hollow Men...Glasgow's Cuban Heels have transformed themselves from a dodgy modish bunch into a far more original funk-inclined group on 'Walk on Water" (Cuba Libre Records). The same year the band had two tracks included on a mini-album 'Second City Statik', on the Statik label, and indeed both Statik and Cuba Libre were more active than Postcard in 1980 & 1981.

Whilst not wishing to diminish the importance of the Postcard label, it's important to note that other labels such as Rational, from Edinburgh, and run by Josef K's manager, Alan Campbell, released excellent singles by the likes of The Delmontes and Article 58, but struggled to gain traction and exposure because of the privileging of the Postcard label. Douglas MacIntyre, felt that 'every label (independent and major) were in the shadows of these labels' (Postcard & Fast) creative output during their short existence'. Despite this, he is still enthusiastic about the era. 'We were very excited when Article 58 signed to Rational and hit it off with label boss Allan Campbell immediately. Their releases by Delmontes, Visitors, Paul Haig/Rhythm of Life etc were great records. Article 58 got great radio support especially from John Peel on BBC Radio 1, and were hipped up by influential journalists at the time such as Dave McCullough at Sounds and Paul Morley at NME. We did interviews with fanzines, but I can't remember which ones! The early 80s was a pivotal period where artists also started self-releasing singles, in Scotland perhaps Fire Engines on their Codex Communication label and the mini-album release on Statik (Second City Statik) featuring Restricted Code, Positive Noise and The Alleged were the most notable'.

Also worth mentioning is Tony Pilley's excellent short lived Edinburgh based label 'Barclay Towers', which released singles by The Brills, the Electric Personalities and Pilley himself, in 1979-80. It also released a compilation LP, 'Scottish Kultchur', with a great and funny sleeve design, featuring Rezillos, Neon Barbs, Another Pretty Face and Boots For Dancing amongst others.

Fanzines, however, continued their infatuation with Postcard records. All Alan Horne's talk of growing and nurturing homegrown talent began to fall apart once Orange Juice moved to a major record label, the latest of a long line of Scottish bands to up sticks and move to the Big Smoke. Stephen Pastel in a later fanzine interview is more ambivalent about the label. 'It was good for Glasgow 'cos up until then you had all the pub bores...but I don't like Josef K and I don't like Aztec Camera.' The latter band were to follow Orange Juice in a move to a major, and Postcard's days were numbered. The Pastels, however, remained in Glasgow, becoming integral to its evolving music scene. By doing this, and not signing to any major labels, it's fair to say that they turned themselves into a viable long term proposition.

Born Yesterday – Editor Unknown.

One earlier issue of *Born Yesterday* contains a hilarious, long and camp interview with Edwyn and Steven of Orange Juice where they relish slagging off Alan Horne and other Glasgow bands – talking of Alan's short lived (and thankfully) ill-fated band Oscar Wild 'all their songs were delivered in a flat monotone, and all the time Alan would be lisping, and Donald would be Kenny Morris from the Banshees, but with a double hernia. They were horrendous, the most horrible group ever.' Edwyn was equally as scathing on Alan's reign as 'Mr Postcard'. 'When Dave McCullough (Sounds Magazine) called him Alan the Cuddly Wee Kid, he started believing his own press. I'm going to make the majors eat shit (Snort! Snort!)'.

John Dingwall of *Stand & Deliver* zine believed that 'Alan Horne was bit of a snob and aloof, and looked down his nose at anything he hadn't been directly involved with. He was an Andy Warhol like figure, almost otherworldly. What he did with Postcard was simply thrilling but I don't think he thought there was a scene and there probably wasn't until Postcard came along and inspired so many other Glasgow bands to pick up guitars and start dressing like they came from the mid-West. Everybody dressed like that for a while thanks to the Briggait market and Flip, a clothing store in Queen Street that bought second hand American clothing in bulk.'

Brian Hogg reminds us of the reality of running an independent label north of the border. 'Alan Horne was a master of promotion, visually and verbally. Although aesthetically and culturally different, both he and Bob Last at Fast had individual takes on the pop process and, for a brief time, each exploited this to the hilt with some success. They were critics' darlings; they used visuals brilliantly and they issued some fabulous records. However, there's only one band which went from Glasgow's Mars Bar to the US stage at Live Aid – Simple Minds. Postcard barely lasted a year; Swamplands, which followed, was commercially unsuccessful - despite its lofty ambition - and Bob soon grew tired of Pop management'.

It's fair to say that The Bluebells came out of the whole Postcard milieu as it was about to disintegrate, and although their single Everybody's Somebody's Fool was catalogued by the label in 1981, it went unreleased. 'Yes, in the early days of The Bluebells we rehearsed and recorded in the Hellfire Club behind the petrol garage on Woodlands Road which was run by Big David Henderson and his girlfriend at the time Jaquie Bradley (Sophisticated Boom Boom/His Latest Flame) explains Ken McCluskey. 'This was the same studio that Aztec Camera and Orange Juice recorded in for a while. Orange Juice's 'Ostrich Churchyard' (an album unreleased at the time) which is one of my favourites, was recorded there with David Henderson. The Postcard guys, especially Edwyn and Alan, encouraged Bobby to start a band and with the help of his friend Gerry McElhone (Altered Images Manager) he put together a band named Oxfam Warriors who maybe played two gigs and kind of fell apart. But that gave him the songwriting bug I think, and he started putting ideas together for a stronger line up'.

'My brother David and I knew Aztec Camera from the Lanarkshire scene and Bobby introduced us to the other Postcardians as he had written a lot about them in his fanzine *Ten Commandments* and had become quite friendly with most of them. The Initial idea was to release a single on Postcard and 'Everybody's Somebody's Fool' was scheduled for a release on the label but by the time we got round to recording it , Aztec Camera had moved on to Rough Trade, Orange Juice had signed to Polydor and Josef K had vanished off the scene so there wasn't much of a Postcard remaining apart from Alan Horne who had an idea for a Postcard International. In the meantime, The Bluebells were invited to support Haircut 100 on tour, and it was on this tour that the media and major label interest started to grow. We eventually signed to London Records which was ideal because we got a wage from that and we were all signing on the dole at the time'.

Other musicians now saw punk as old hat, and only a few bands from that era were held up as being 'pop' enough to point the way forward. Ken Popple from the band Biff Bang Pow mused to *Slow Dazzle* that 'I know people in New Zealand who think the same way. I mean, they'll never forget bands like the Buzzcocks or The Ramones'. The sadly missed Tommy Cherry of Glasgow's psychedelic funsters, The Bachelor Pad, stated about their music in 1985 that 'Oh gosh! I think (David Harris) got it right when he said it was a head-on collision between The Buzzcocks and Syd Barrett'.

And Andrew Burnett from Paisley's Close Lobsters sums up this 'better' interpretation of punk. 'We met when we were at school, all involved in punk rock and its post-punk aftermaths – the real punk rock, not the one where people took it literally and uncritically, not the popular perception of leather jackets, mohawks, spitting and touristy attractions etc. So, we were destined in a way to do it given our collective belief in the spirit of punk rock. The late 70s was magical for music'. The band members had put together a fanzine called *Ferocious Apache*, which was informed by the preceding punk era, 'it was on the cusp of post-punk and the radical pop thing. We were as much influenced by *Vague* fanzine with its focus on Situationism and Flesh for Lulu and the Southern Death Cult. As we developed the group we liked to put our influences as Crass and Orange Juice. Also *Juniper Beri Beri* was very much of what we considered to be our natural constituency, along with *Attack on Bzag* and *Slow Dazzle*.

Ferocious Apache – Courtesy Andrew Burnett.

Ken McCluskey believes that punk had been a breath of fresh air, but that 'It did however start to decay quite quickly with folk throwing their weight about and accusing youngsters of being 'plastic Punks' and 'Too posh to be a Punk', not street enough etc. A bit like Lord of The Flies. Then politics got into it. You could be a left wing punk or a right wing punk, and eventually ugly fascist skinheads appeared on the scene as some throwback to the arse end of the 60's. And then the glue sniffing mohican tramp brigade with dogs on a string began to extort money from the younger ones. It was all over quite quickly, but the initial vibe was really inspirational and opened up a lot of folks minds to what was actually possible. It was certainly where the seeds of the Bluebells were planted'. But much like Orange Juice, there were other influences which the band were able to incorporate into their sound. 'Bobby being a bit older was into 1960's garage bands and would make tapes of The Pebbles compilations and The VU, Byrds, Buffalo Springfield, Bob Dylan and The Band, The Faces, Sly and The Family Stone. David and I had heard a lot of this from our older siblings previously, so it felt natural just like a reawakening. The Monkees were also a big influence'.

Juniper Beri-Beri felt that the original spirit of punk was dead, and posited the idea of starting something new up, but was unsure as to what that might be, and Stephen Pastel confirms today that the after-Postcard period was 'quite strange'. What might this scene potentially look like?

Certainly, in Scotland a raft of bands formed in the wake of Postcard's demise, upholding its rattly amateurisms -Stephen Pastel described how he 'didn't like a lot of other music that was coming out of Scotland – and we wanted to do something more naïve' - the irony being that Postcard wanted to be professional in infiltrating the 'proper' pop charts – but its bands only found fame and fortune by signing to major labels, a good example being Orange Juice signing to Polydor Records and enjoying a UK Top Ten hit with 'Rip it Up And Start Again'. Stephen says that he loved Orange Juice more than Postcard itself, and that of the bands around in the wake of the label's demise, 'Strawberry Switchblade had the most commercial potential. I really love their first single 'Trees and Flowers'. And, Strawberry Switchblade being a case in point, success wasn't always the best outcome for bands who might have been playing in front of three students and a dog before they got signed. 'The advantage us and The Pastels have had over other bands is maybe that we've not had that much success', recalled the BMX Bandits' Duglas Stewart in 1996, 'things like money and the press paying a lot of attention, most people find hard'. As noted earlier perhaps there is a good case to be made for the Pastels being the first of the after-punk bands to demonstrate that you could both remain independent, and base yourself in Scotland. 'We didn't want to move to London' asserts Stephen, 'and staying in Glasgow allowed us time to develop along our own path.'

....

If you take a look at CD 3 from Cherry Red's excellent compilation 'Big Gold Dreams: A Story Of Scottish Independent Music 1977-1989 5CD Boxset', they are a virtual template for the indie music of the 1980s

1. FEATHERS OAR-BLADES – Cocteau Twins

2. OUT OF NOWHERE – The Twinsets

3. CATH – The Bluebells

4. A GIRL CALLED JOHNNY – The Waterboys

5. LUCKY STAR (Moonboot Version) – Friends Again

6. TREES AND FLOWERS (92 Happy Customers Version) – Strawberry Switchblade

7. SIXTEEN REASONS – Jazzateers

8. STOP THE RAIN – The Suede Crocodiles

9. FLOWERS IN THE SKY – The Revolving Paint Dream

10. THINK! – Jasmine Minks

11. THERE MUST BE A BETTER LIFE – Biff Bang Pow!

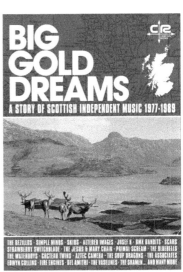

Big Gold Dreams Courtesy Cherry Red Records.

12. ALL I NEED IS EVERYTHING – Aztec Camera

13. OVER YOUR SHOULDER – Pop Wallpaper

14. DREAMING – The Wee Cherubs

15. CATHEDRAL – Fini Tribe

16. UPSIDE DOWN – The Jesus And Mary Chain

17. BABY HONEY   The Pastels

18. YOU SUPPLY THE ROSES – Memphis

19. AIN'T THAT ALWAYS THE WAY – Paul Quinn

20. UNAMERICAN BROADCASTING – Win

21. SWALLOW – Blood Uncles

Simon Reynolds speaking in the Big Gold Dream film, said that with reference to the emergence of Postcard Records and beyond, 'what we now know as indie music was invented in Scotland'. Without a doubt, the musical output from that as evidenced in the tracklisting above, makes for a convincing argument. The pop sensibility of bands like Orange Juice, Josef K and Postcard's other artists (mixed up with influences like the Velvet Underground's third album) created a distinctive strand of post-punk that evolved into indie rock and pop in the 1980s. Postcard's releases featured distinctive artwork, posters and inserts that also influenced future indie labels like Sarah Records. But as mentioned above, it's important not to forget the about of bands on Statik, Rational, and Cuba Libre, as well as Fast Product's successor, Pop:Aural, who helped to shape the pop underground in Scotland.

A load of fanzines emerged to document the indie scene of the period such as *Baby Honey, Bam, Deadbeat, Falling & Laughing, Ferocious Apache, Inside Out*, and more. There was also space provided for bands outside the Central Belt – This Poison from Perth, The Shamen & The Jasmine Minks from Aberdeen, The Big Gun from Irvine. Tommy Cherry again summed up the fanzine spirit of the day, '...it was like punk but with groovy Warhol kids instead of all those lumpy Clash fans and Sid idiots'.

···

Twenty miles down the River Clyde from Glasgow, towards the sea, lie the post-industrial towns of Inverclyde – Port Glasgow and Greenock. In the mid-'80s, there were several dedicated individuals determined to promote music in their area to the same degree as their big-city neighbours. Chris Davidson was one of those individuals. 'I had an idea around 1983 to create a local music fanzine. I placed an ad on the wall of Rhythmic Records asking if anybody would like to meet to discuss contributing articles on music, film, books, politics, football, fashion etc. Loads turned up at the meeting...and the contributors were enigmatically known as the

Politburo!' *Slow Dazzle* sold extremely well, with the first issue in 1984 selling out all 300 copies produced. Issue 5 had The Pastels on the cover, and Chris smiles at the recollection that the interview with Stephen Pastel was only granted on that particular proviso. 'Well, no one else would put us on their front page', asserts Stephen today, but laughs in recognition of the ambition behind that.

One of the bands uniting these diverse spirits were the original punky shamblers, the Television Personalities, fronted by the inimitable Dan Treacy. Again, another band directly in thrall to the 60s, albeit one where the 'Nuggets' bands had ruled the pop charts, rather than the Beatles.

'Six months ago I couldn't've told you a thing about The Television Personalities' ran a feature in *Slow Dazzle.*' I hadn't heard of them since the days of the 'Bill Grundy' and 'Syd Barrett' singles, and didn't even know if they still existed. Then I started to read some great new (and not so new) fanzines which all referred to the T.V.Ps as some sort of seminal influence, heard the 'Sense Of Belonging' single, and slowly got hooked. The clincher was when I got my mitts on a fanzine from East Kilbride called *Bombs Away Batman* which suggested that life wasn't worth living until you'd heard an L.P. by the Personalities called ' They Could Have Been Bigger Than The Beatles'. A title like that, and a review written with such passion and enthusiasm sent me rushing down to Rhythmic Records to order it, and three days later I too was drooling over this masterpiece. I had to hear more, so it wasn't long before I'd tracked down the 2nd L.P. 'Mummy You're Not Watching Me' and the latest one 'The Painted Word', both of which are equally brilliant. Out of the blue I'd found my new 'favourite group in the whole world' (for this month at least!) so you could imagine the elation I felt when co-incidentally their first ever tour of Northern Britain was announced. Newcastle and Dundee were cancelled (as a result of a fire at the club in Dundee) and I eventually caught up with them at the Heathery Bar in Wishaw'.

'I'd expected to see four or five people on stage and wondered at first if only three could re-create the recorded works. Of course they could. To say that they were magnificent would be an understatement. 'Hello, we're The T.V. Personalities, and this is 'Three Wishes'' was the introduction to a mesmerising set of songs, mostly familiar, climaxing with an extended version of 'David Hockney's Diary' into which was thrown snippets of everything: from Frankie Goes To Mothercare, Pink Floyd, The Beatles, Velvets, Human League, Smiths, Thompson Twins, Troggs, Jonathan Richman, ? And The Mysterians, Siouxsie, Divine, Evelyn Thomas, The Who, in fact anything which came into Dan's vivid inspiration. Don't waste your money on the new Public Image L.P. - take a risk and buy one of Dan's!')

43

This obsessive 'fandom' of bands was reiterated by Stephen Pastel, emphasizing the 'fan' aspect of fanzines in his interview with *Slow Dazzle*. '..at their best, it's just people sitting around who put their opinions down, get the thing printed themselves...suppose you really like the records, why should you pretend you don't like them? Why should you slag half of them off?'. That's exactly what the mainstream music press were constantly doing. Introducing its readership to bands, promoting them, and then deciding that they didn't like them, and then unfairly criticising them.

The final issue of *Slow Dazzle* came out a mere 10 months after the first, and Chris admits that this amazing burst of creativity nearly finished him off! Featuring a Jesus and Mary Chain interview and the first feature on Creation Records, with a cartoon cover of the band drawn by Stingrytes frontman George Miller, it sold a massive 1,200 copies, 'largely due to getting rave reviews in NME, Sounds, Melody Maker, and Billy Sloan (Radio Clyde) & John Peel on Radio 1'. Chris says that reason he managed to interview both the Mary Chain and Alan MacGee's Creation records mob, was that it was the Creation showcase at The Venue in Glasgow. 'A real exclusive that. The world's first Mary Chain interview!' Stephen Pastel remains convinced that his zine was there before *Slow Dazzle*, but acknowledges that Chris probably published the interview before him.

And about that interview, Chris dispels the myth that they were uncooperative. 'We were sitting on the back stairs, and I was winding the interview up, when I realised that I hadn't pressed 'record' on my tape recorder! 'Nae worries' says Jim Reid, and we did it all again....' The band themselves were happy to big themselves up, not that they needed to, as *Slow Dazzle's* reviewer summarily dismissed the other bands like Biff Bang Pow as an 'unfunny joke'. But as for the self-proclaimed 'best band in the world' it was a different matter. 'Like the Sex Pistols in '76, it wasn't really the music, or whether you think it was good or bad that matters. It's the fact that this band exists!'

Slow Dazzle Creation Records Collage – courtesy Chris Davidson.

Strangely, for a band who always proclaimed all their contemporaries to be rubbish, William Reid was complimentary about some Scottish bands when interviewed by *Slow Dazzle*, admitting that he 'liked the ones that are influenced by the Velvet Underground. Orange Juice. Pastels. I like some Fire Engines' records, and Primal Scream and Meat Whiplash'. But then he ruined it all by going on to say, 'I can't stand Aztec Camera. Roddy Frame's so pre-punk isn't he? The new Strawberry Switchblade record's crap'.

Slow Dazzle Issue 6 Mary Chain Cover courtesy of Chris Davidson.

Chris went on to set up a club night in the town called Subterraneans, which brought bands like The Pastels, Soup Dragons, Close Lobsters & Marc Riley's Creepers to play in Greenock. 'One of the most pleasant surprises was the night that Nikki Sudden turned up with Roland S Howard from the Birthday Party on guitar and Lindy Morrison from the Go Betweens on drums! Brilliant'

Chapter 4 :

C30-C60-C-90 Go!

KBD 4 Cassette – Courtesy Michael Train.

During the 1980's, the major UK music papers like NME, Melody Maker and Sounds regularly produced cover-mounted cassettes featuring a mixture of up and coming bands with more established artists. The NME also published the C-81 cassette, which is maybe the highwater mark of the cassette underground moving overground, into the mainstream.

The cassette started being an important medium in the late '70s with the arrival of the Walkman and in-car tape players, allowing music to become ubiquitous in a way that vinyl couldn't. I remember kids in school taking tapes and cheap mono cassette recorders in so that we could listen to them. I was introduced to bands like Simple Minds, the Psychedelic Furs, Spear of Destiny and others on tape first. It enabled us, and other kids with guitars to record home 'demos' and really opened up a whole new world. In a remote location such as Skye, cassettes came into their own as you could mail order tapes from magazines more cheaply and easily than records. Compilations were made and shared, cover art was designed, and I'm convinced that these activities spurred some of the more creative minds to move into other areas of music and design.

The cassette as a format had been around for a decade, but the tipping point, as it was also for fanzines, was the upsurge in the number of bands in the wake of punk. Punk had imbued potential musicians, writers & label owners with a sense of purpose. A DIY spirit that fanzines, indie labels and bands releasing their own music made creating an artifact a distinct possibility.

For musicians, the cassette was the great enabler. For aspiring writers, it was cheap photocopying, allowing for similar low volume production, as required. Another reason for the popularity of cassettes as a DIY medium

46

was their ease and cheapness of posting them compared to vinyl. Following this logic, at the outer edges of the DIY universe lurked the cassette labels, and bands who released their songs on tapes, either because of cost or adherence to the independent ethos. A number of these cassette bands, like Dundee's Scrotum Poles, were kicking about on the Scottish scene in the early '80s, and one of the most interesting cassette labels was *Deadbeat*, started in Edinburgh by Vinny Bee as an offshoot of the fanzine with the same name. 'We made a run of only 100 and sold them for two pounds. The next two tapes, with the original titles *Deadbeat* 2 & 3 came out in 1984 and 1985. I thought all the bands deserved to be heard and this format worked well for them all. I gave copies to London A & R folk who were always on the lookout but mostly the bands got gigs from the extra publicity and that was the main thing.'

Megazine – Courtesy Brian Speedie.

Scrotum Poles E.P – courtesy of Brian Speedie.

The aforementioned Scrotum Poles set up their own cassette label, One Tone records, and ran off 100 copies of their 'Auchmithie Calling' in 1979, via a pal at Dundee College of Education, for which according to the Poles' Craig Methven, 'he may have been paid in pints!' As well as production, the artwork was DIY. 'We photocopied the covers because we couldn't afford to print them, and then glued them in my Mum's kitchen'. They also released an E.P on vinyl, some copies of which found their way onto the *Megazine* fanzine from Stirling. Brian Speedie from the zine knew Glen Connell, who played with The Scrotes as they were affectionately called, and he suggested the link with the fanzine. 'We made the cover and my mum wrote happy and sad on each side of the disc. We gave it away with issue two'.

Michael Train recalls both the E.P and cassette fondly. 'Radio Tay' was the first Poles I ever heard, and that buzzing guitar is still great. It was on a 'Back To Front' compilation that I had to mail-order from Germany to our tiny village of Seal Cove, Maine. I heard the band name long before I ever heard the music!

Pungent Records, which was affiliated with *Fumes* fanzine in Glasgow, brought out a home-made tape compilation in 1980 called 'Urban Development', which featured an early incarnation of Aztec Camera, Positve Noise, and The Unknowns amongst others. A second compilation came out later in the year featuring the delights of Johnny Yen, Subtle Props and Facial Hair. They were both given away free with the zine.

Stirling based anarcho-punks, Political Asylum, recorded their self-released and self-duplicated cassette across two days in 1983. Via a network of fanzines, gigs and cassette trading networks, they ended up selling a more than respectable 6,000 copies.

However, it wasn't all indie guitar music that was being released. Glasgow based electronics pioneer Alistair Robertson started producing synth based music in the late '70s. In 1980 he was running his own tape label called Synthetic Tapes which released several of his projects under different names such as DC3, The Written Text and The Klingons. At the same time he joined Stirling based Band Final Program who had formed in 1978, quickly becoming fully synth based and releasing the 7-inch EP 'Protect and Survive' on their own Motion label. Their synth-bass player was called Anne Droid – which is reason enough to seek out their recorded output.

In late 1980 Alistair got to know Ian Dobson (Those Little Aliens) of the Flowmotion Label and wrote several articles for Ian's early *Flowmotion* magazines which also resulted in the release of a solo tape 'The Axe gets Axed' in 1981 as well as a collaboration cassette with Ian Dobson under the name Inter City Static. With support of Mario D'Agostino who produced music under the name Dick Tracy, Roberston produced a second Klingons tape which was released on Synthetic Tapes.

Robert Rental & Thomas Leer were Port Glasgow lads, who had messed about with electronic sounds pre-punk, but it was only following a move to London during punk that they decided to try their hand at some primitive home recording. Although they self-released singles independently – Robert's 'Paralysis' and Thomas' 'Private Plane, it was on the same cheap equipment lugged across London from one flat to another. With 'Private Plane' receiving Single of the Week in NME, and runs of both records selling out, this ultimately led to the recording of the collaborative album, 'From The Port to The Bridge', which went on to sell over 7,000 copies over the next 9 months. Writer Simon Dell approached the Beacon Arts Centre in Greenock in 2016 with the idea of doing an exhibition. The exhibition eventually came together in 2018 and ran for 4 weeks. 'I wrote the booklet, 'From The Bridge to The Port' to coincide, along with postcard sets, posters, t-shirts. I was keen to take the exhibition to London, as that was where Thomas and Robert mainly did their musical work, and I finally got support from Mute Records as they were reissuing The Bridge We ran the exhibition at the Horse Hospital in central London for 3 weeks'.

In 1980, the NME had started a column to cover the proliferating cassette scene, but only ten months later abruptly stopped publishing it. Critics lost patience quite suddenly with the aural tape oddities which they only recently championed. One possible on the reason for that was, that the record industry, slightly miffed at the whole home taping malarky, had warned off the music press that advertising may be cut if the cassette scene coverage continued. 'Home taping is killing music' was the ominous cry from the major labels...... Whatever the case, a gap in the market opened up for bands who had not yet been signed to labels, but were ambitious enough to do so, and that is where cassette-zines were able to tap into that demand.

....

Fast forward to December 1982 on the Isle of Skye. I'm finishing up for the Christmas school holidays. Probably listening to The Jam or something. At the same time on the Glasgow to London sleeper, Robert H King and his pal Elliot are sitting with boxes of cassettes, 1000 to be precise, info sheets, photos envelopes and glue pens. Excitedly folding, glueing and packing the first edition of *Pleasantly Surprised*, billing itself as Scotland's first audio-zine, although this seems a slightly disingenuous description, as Elliot's *Sunset Gun* had come out a year earlier.

'My original idea in 1980 was to start a fanzine', says Robert. 'I had been buying stacks of them that were doing the rounds at the time, and it looked easy enough to do. I had been given a lot of info from themselves had been inspired by the inclusion of a breakdown in costs and manufacturing details in Scritti Politti's 'Skank Bloc Bologna' EP'. Following a Clash gig at the Glasgow Apollo, Robert chatted to Joe Strummer and told him that he was thinking of starting a fanzine. Joe's response was 'you can't change anything by just thinking about it. You just have to do it yourself'.

Suitably inspired he began to write to the bands he liked, and he soon amassed both a large number of interviews and also cassettes that the bands had sent back to him. 'It occurred to me that I should put together a compilation and let people hear this stuff for themselves'. He mentioned his idea to a friend in Bloggs record shop in Glasgow, and they decided to work together on the project. That friend turned out to be Elliot Davis, future manager of Wet Wet Wet, who had brought out the *Sunset Gun* zine, as mentioned above and its attendant cassette zine the previous year (under the guise of Klark Kent – not the Stewart Copeland nom de plume!). The cassette zine featured the likes of Altered Images, H20 and The Poems.

The resulting collaboration between Robert and Elliot featured material from Cocteau Twins, Billy MacKenzie, The Wake and Primal Scream amongst others. 'When we arrived in London, we made our way across town to Rough Trade. Geoff (Travis) put it on the tape deck and looked over the packaging. "I'll take 800 and pay you in 30 days". Geoff advised that we manufacture more and gave us contact details for Fast Forward in Edinburgh, a small distribution company initially set up by Bob Last'.

Sandy MacLean of The Cartel network offered the lads a distribution deal, and the cassette got radio play from John Peel and Billy Sloan on Radio Clyde, as well as good reviews in the music papers. 'Sandy encouraged us to pursue further editions, and so our second issue took place within a few months, and we had so much material from Bauhaus, Nico, Primevals, Blue Orchids etc that it ended up as a 2 x C60 cassette with a 28 page publication'.

After the release of *Pleasantly Surprised* Issue 2 'The Angels Are Coming', Robert and Elliot went their separate ways. 'We parted company, and so the money was halved.' With a new enthusiasm and donations from a few friends, Robert carried on with great success. At the label's peak, 5000 copies of *Pleasantly Surprised* Issue 5 were sold.

The cassettes were all elaborately packaged, usually with oversized cardboard covers in plastic sleeves and including several inserts or booklets. The music was mostly made up of demo, live or alternate take recordings which gave music fans a great opportunity to hear their favourite bands in a different light. In addition to offering compilations of otherwise unheard material, *Pleasantly Surprised* had the opportunity to release entire collections of rare music by Band Of Holy Joy, Test Dept, God's Gift, Clair Obscur, Dif Juz, and Dance Chapter.

Of course, not everyone bought into the cassette revolution. Joe Foster of Creation Records told *Slow Dazzle* that 'every single has to be a total package, that's why people don't buy cassettes. It's just a piece of plastic. You play it, and that's it'. He obviously had never seen *Pleasantly Surprised.*

Marc Masters, author of 'High Bias: The Distorted History of the Cassette Tape', recognizes the synergy between music zines and audio cassettes. 'Tapes and zines were definitely very aligned in terms of zines reviewing tapes and people collecting both. Often zines would have specific columns covering cassette releases, but also many of them covered cassettes in a regular capacity just like they covered vinyl releases'. And he emphasises the importance of the aspect of portability as well. 'Tapes were certainly like zines in the way it was easy to make them on your own and distribute them through the mail, without the expense or the time commitment of pressing records'.

Simply Thrilled edited by Jim from Glasgow.

Fanzines that were not specifically audio zines were often giving away free tapes or flexi Discs, such as *Skipping Kitten* which gave away a free Shamen flexi, and *Simply Thrilled*, a 7" sized zine with a great free flexi featuring the Bachelor Pad and Baby Lemonade. One of the most important 'freebie cassettes of the 1980s was *Honey At The Core*, given away by the eponymously named zine in 1986. The next chapter will take a closer look at that, along with the C86 cassette.

Stand and Deliver zine, edited by John Dingwall, had earlier given away the first recordings by Del Amitri and The Bluebells as a free flexi disc before they had official label releases. 'The decision to start the fanzine was spontaneous. I was at a gig at the Glasgow College of Technology which was a double header featuring The Fall and The Cramps. A great gig. I was there with friends Dee and Sock. Dee ran the Scottish fan club for The Cure and it was Sock who said, after The Fall had played, "Why don't we start a fanzine?" The power of youth is you don't overthink things. We traipsed backstage and interviewed Mark E Smith of The Fall and Lux Interior of The Cramps. I had grown up reading NME because I had a paper run delivering Evening Times. I delivered 55 Evening Times and one NME which I read by the time it was delivered to the owner. I only became aware of other fanzines like *Ten Commandments and Sniffin' Glue* after I started *Stand & Deliver*."

Fanzine freebies now attract ridiculous sums of money online and John contrasts the wide eyed idealism of an indie kid with the collector culture of today. 'Yeah, the first issue we printed 100 copies which sold out on the first day so we printed another 90. We were really surprised that people bought it. The biggest selling issue was the last one with the Del Amitri and Bluebells flexidisc. I borrowed my aunt's car and drove to London. Rough Trade records and distribution took a bunch which went around the world and I stopped off at record shops on the way back up the road at places like Coventry and Birmingham. I think we pressed up 1,000 if memory serves me but only 750 had the flexi. Someone offered me £500 for the flexi recently but I don't even have copies of the fanzines'.

And on that zine name, he has this to say. 'Sock had come up with idea to call the zine *Stand And Deliver'*. One of the team subsequently interviewed Adam Ant, and six months later he released a single with the same name. I was a bit miffed because I didn't want people thinking we had taken the name from a pop act. I'm still not entirely over it, but I suppose with his dandy highwayman persona, it was too good a trick to miss.'

Moving into the '90s, there was still a strong cassette trading and label scene both in Scotland and UK wide. Mark Ritchie, who set up his fanzine *Splish! Splash!* Splosh! as a schoolboy in South Lanarkshire, was part of that scene. 'Just in terms of trading tapes through the post, that was happening constantly, and I wrote to so many people, and got to hear so much music that way. 'Bi-Joopiter' was the first actual tape label I remember from the UK at the time. Then there were the labels that put out compilations like 'Something's Burning in Paradise', which we had a song on. 'Glidge' and 'Bliss' were another couple of good ones that came later. I also used to trade tapes with labels like 'Matching Head', who released experimental/noise stuff, though I was probably more into the American tape labels 'Blackbean' and 'Placenta' and Don Campau's 'Lonely Whistle'. Don also did a cool radio show which would play all kinds of obscure underground stuff, including my music. In terms of Scotland: I'm not sure they had an official label, but I loved the self-released tapes by the Larkhall band Remember Fun. They were rather influenced by the Smiths, who were probably the band that got me into 'indie' music in the first place'.

Mark eventually moved into setting up his own cassette label, KAW (Killing Animals Is Wrong), in order to get his own music out into the world, but ended up diversifying by 'releasing stuff by our friends' bands, like Rentboy and Grrr! from Middlesbrough, and compilations featuring all kinds of groovy people such as the Siddeleys, BMX Bandits, Pink Kross, Valenstar, Pansy Division and Mogwai. We also put out a 7" by a guy called Timo as well as the Shy Rights Movement single'.

Bosque Records, a Glasgow based DIY label putting out the '90s version of punk rock and noise was run by Tom Worthington. Although not specifically a 'tape' label, they put out quite a few cassette releases. 'It was a low stakes, cheap way of distributing music, but real and easy to sell at gigs. It also nicely aligned/linked up with our use of cassette tape loops and 4-track recorders. I used to trade tapes with any and everyone and we'd often get sent music on cassette for the label, gigs etc. Cheap and easy to send overseas as well – a huge positive of the format. And of course lots of these people were doing zines and we were sending them artwork, words and music for said zines in return'.

Chapter 5 :

Safety Nets and Jingly Creeps

Back to 1986 now. I'm sitting listening to the Rain Parade's 'Explosions in The Glass Palace' in the sun with my legs dangling over our peat bank, waiting to help out with the lifting and stacking. That was a champagne year. The year I learned to drive. The year I got my exam results. The year I left school. The year I heard the fabulous Shop Assistants! The year of...... .....ssh! Whisper it. The NME's C86 cassette............

Roy Carr of the NME explained the cassette's origins. 'We thought we'd do one of these for what was happening in indie music at the time. I'd done it for the paper before in 1981 – the imaginatively titled C81 – and that had been quite popular. So, a few of us got together and started picking the bands we wanted to go on the tape.' At the time, the NME was fond of putting together and releasing compilation tapes covering any number of different genres. It might sound quaint today in an age of unfettered access to anything ever recorded, but in those far off days a simple compilation tape could be one of the best chances for its readers to get hold of something new.

What it did have was something to suit every indie kid's taste. From the lumpy super-speed guitar angst of the Wedding Present, to the souped up Soup Dragons' Buzzcocks riffs . From the Beeheart-lite of the MacKenzies, to the Syd Barrett-isms of The Servants, this was the first time, for me anyway, I had ever seen a proper 'indie' compilation, as opposed to one your mates had knocked up on a C60 tape. Referring to the Soup Dragons, my favourite quip about them came from a fan in London, 'They were still Buzzcocks wannabes. Their amps kept dying on them and the Dingwalls crowd shouted 'Something's Gone Wrong Again!" My group of friends christened them the 'Soupcocks' when we first heard them, but drummer Ross Sinclair finds it funny that the Buzzcocks comparisons persist as he was the only band member who drew his inspiration from that particular band. 'The Buzzcocks and The Who. The rest of the band's influence were much more diverse.'

One of the most interesting back stories of the C86 tape is that of Sushil K. Dade. Sushil was editing his own fanzine, *Pure Popcorn* when he put up a notice in a music shop in Glasgow saying that he was looking to join a band. Sean Dickson answered, and the Soup Dragons started to coalesce. 'I'd started Art School in 1984', says Ross, and I was playing in a band called 'Gods For All Occasions', that featured Raymond McGinlay. We played a gig in the Vic Bar in the Art School, and Sean Dickson was there. He said he was looking for a drummer, even though I was playing guitar. Our other guitarist was away, and Jim McCullough came in, and I switched to drums, and that was us ready'. For their first gig the band supported Primal Scream at the legendary Splash 1 club, organized by Bobby Gillespie amongst others, where the DJs played compilation cassettes rather than vinyl singles. Ross acknowledges the importance of clubs like that in fostering a belief that you could do it yourself. 'Splash 1 was really important for Glasgow and that group of people who went there became musicians, and visual artists etc. There was a feeling you didn't have to go down to London and go through the sausage machine. Bands like the Pastels fostered a mutually supportive scene in the city'.

Sushil himself was an enthusiastic reader of the fanzines being produced in Scotland at that time, and reckons that the two exceptional ones were *Juniper Beri Beri* and *Slow Dazzle*. 'They took a lot of care in presenting a fanzine with maximum creativity and great illustrations and art which I found really inspiring'. His own musical influences were diverse, and he was discovering acts as diverse as Kraftwerk to Ravi Shankar and Orange Juice via The Pastels to Black Uhuru.

Courtesy Sushil K Dade.

The community aspect of producing a zine was important to him as well, 'our main point of contact was selling at gigs in a carrier bag or distributing on foot to book/record shops, so it what a great way of meeting like minded people or those who provided a framework of support by stocking in their shops. Word of mouth was very powerful and the message would spread. This is pre-internet and wider exposure was only possible occasionally and came later on the radio or music press'.

That exposure came quickly, as the baby Dragons, barely out of nappies, recorded a track 'If You Were The Only Girl In The World, (Would You Take Me?)' with the intent of releasing it as a flexi with the zine. It became the NME's single of the week (perhaps the only one ever?), and before they had time to book their seats on the overnight bus, they were heading to London to do a Radio 1 session. They were then invited to contribute a track to the NME C86 cassette, and the rest, as they say, is history. Duglas Stewart of the BMX Bandits recalled in 1995 how Sean was put under immense pressure after that review stated that 'it was the best ever record made'. The irony being that arguably the most 'C86' of all the bands didn't get a track on the cassette. 'We actually got the opposite in our review in Sounds', he laughs 'they said it was without doubt the worst single of all time."

Some of the bands ended up on the tape accidentally, like the Close Lobsters. Andrew Burnett acknowledges this fact when asked how his band ended up on the tape 'I can only assume by accident. A good friend Jon Hunter, trumpet player with the June Brides took us under his wing and promoted the band in London for a while. I'm sure it was his influence that helped bring about the inclusion on C86. The June Brides were our heroes!'

Despite the differing and disparate styles on display, pretty soon most writers and critics were knocking the tape as a sugary repository of tweeness to be well and truly slagged off; shy boys (and girls) with glasses and pimply skin singing about their lovelorn lives over a 3-chord strum. A badly played fey-whey cake mixture of songs which sounded somewhere between underperforming Byrds B-sides and Orange juice outtakes. Simon Reynolds, curtly dismissed the whole 'scene' as 'Anoraksia Nervosa'!

What all these older writers seemed to forget, was that us kids of 16 and 17 who bought and listened to the C86 tunes, were too young to remember punk, and had probably missed the boat on post-punk too, so some of the antecedents were lost in translation, or simply not understood. NME scribe David Quantick 'hated indie, and I hated C86'. Fellow writer Hoskyns called it a 'load of junk'. But, Hoskyns was 27 at the time. Even if I had read what he said, I would not have cared a jot. It's easy to be sneery when you've lived through the post punk era of great music, but I'd literally never heard Orange Juice by that point, so the music seemed to be new for our generation. In retrospect when you delved into a bit of research a few years later the whole Byrds/Who/Barrett/Beefheart/Buzzcocks/OJ continuum was laid obviously bare, but at the time, who cared. At least Reynolds does acknowledge that the androgyny and sexual politics of the so called 'C-86 or 'shambling' scenes would 'form the basis of Riot Grrrl a decade later', so there is a worthwhile and lasting legacy to a sadly derided era of indie-pop. And there has been a surprising amount of recent interest which has built up around the tape in the intervening years. Witness Nige Tassell's book 'Whatever Happened to The C86 Kids?', where he embarked on a journey to track down a member of each band who had contributed to the tape.

The Close Lobsters were shambling too, but only after a few beers that 'once had Alan McGhee reprimand us for denigrating comments about the twee scene. I kept my mouth shut because we were on the guest list for the seminal 1985 JAMC show at The Venue in Glasgow and didn't want to jeopardise that. Similarly, we were regularly chastised by C86-ers for our penchant for 'fawing aboot hauf jaked' onstage so to speak. A characteristic pioneered by the Jesus and Mary Chain!'

One of the best bands on the compilation were Edinburgh's Shop Assistants. Although the track on the album is the gauzy, wistful 'It's Up To You', their best song came in the form of an A-side called 'Safety Net'. It was a 12" missive of fuzzy delight, which was bought by the Dunvegan lads on one of their lifeline convoys to the bright lights of Inverness. In a plastic carrier bag containing such delights as the 'Sunny Sundae Smile' E.P by My Bloody Valentine, and the June Brides album, came a single recorded at Pier House Studio in Edinburgh. Kicking off with a barrage of floor toms and ridiculously overloaded bass, the guitar, courtesy of Ramones-nut David Keegan, crashes in with a stupendously fuzzy-but-catchy riff. And on top of that, were sugar sweet vocals from front woman, the late lamented Alex Taylor. I thought it was 'Teenage Kicks' for my generation.

Edinburgh's Shop Assistants in 1985 – Photographer unknown.

And I wasn't alone. It was described by David Sheridan of Trouser Press as 'nothing short of brilliant'. The record was the first release on Keegan & fellow Ramones -nut Stephen Pastel's 53rd & 3rd Records (naturally), and David describes the genesis of the song emerging in the Highlands. 'I wrote the music for Safety Net at my parents' house in Newtonmore early February 1984. The verse part was inspired by the Pastels "Something Going On" from their 1st John Peel Session and there's bits of the Ramones, Rolling Stones (the bass!) VU (the drums!) and the twiddly guitar at the end is inspired by the Squires "Go Ahead" on one of the Pebbles compilations (which were major currency in 1980s Edinburgh)'. The band knew that they had something good in their hands, 'By the time we did Safety Net /Somewhere in China/Almost Made It, we'd played live quite a bit and done a John Peel session so we were more than ready when 'All Day Long' (previous single) was recorded. Alex said "that's the next single" – and it was'.

In considerable contrast to C-86, the other significant compilation cassette from 1986 was one given away by a Glasgow fanzine called *Honey At The Core*. The tape carried the same name as the zine, and was put together by future journalist & music manager, John Williamson. The name was taken from a song by the band Friends Again, and the bands on the tape were essentially the Scottish hitmakers of the next few years – Wet Wet Wet, Hue & Cry, Deacon Blue and The Bluebells amongst others. In her NME review, Lucy Miller summed the majority of bands whose 'smooth pop sensibilities see them lusting after the coffers of major record companies....those expecting a Glasgow tape to be all Soup Dragons and BMX Bandits, Close Lobsters and second rate Mary Chain will be disappointed'. The every independently minded Stephen Pastel opined that 'a lot of the bands in the Eighties were incredibly careerist, stampeding over each other to get to the treasure chest'

Honey At The Core Cassette copyright John Williamson.

John Williamson is clear that he wasn't deliberately trying to make a more 'commercial' compilation, 'I certainly wasn't thinking in silos or genres – it was just what I knew at the time and who said yes. I knew a few of the bands from reading the music press and did ask a couple who appeared on C-86 who, for whatever reason, didn't want to or couldn't contribute a track.' But that misconception became amplified by the music press. 'I guess it could have turned out very differently. The reviews of the cassette in both the NME and Melody Maker both presented it as some kind of antidote to C-86 which may have led to this perception, but definitely not part of any plan on my part'.

His inspiration for putting together the zine and the cassette was a case of happenstance. 'I had left school on 1986, and had a place at university for the following year but was suffering from some form of ME virus that floored me. Putting the cassette together was just something to do to reconnect with the world, though I probably didn't realise that at the time. I hadn't really done a fanzine before, but I had volunteered at a community project / library in Castlemilk and as part of that wrote and edited magazines that covered things that were going on there – music, films, games, sport, a variety of things. Apart from being extremely encouraging they had the best photocopier I had ever seen, and I had access to it. The means of production and all that. . .'

'It also meant that I started to go to gigs regularly in 1985 and for the first time was really aware of what was going on locally in pubs and clubs. I'd always been interested in music, but I guess I didn't know too much about it beyond what I saw on Top of the Pops or what was in the charts. But I'd seen enough and spoken to enough people to get a sense that it was something I wanted to be around or be part of'. This new found interest in music allowed John to be refreshingly eclectic in his tastes. 'I genuinely liked both Wet Wet Wet and the Jesus and Mary Chain and, at the time, couldn't really understand why this was unusual'.

Ken McCluskey recalls John as a genuine music fan, 'always at gigs in Glasgow. He was a fairly quiet guy but he had a great musical knowledge and he asked me one day for a track for a compilation he was releasing with his fanzine *Honey at The Core*. I gave him a copy of a song I had written for The Bluebells named 'Guns and Accordians' The song was about all the outmoded sectarian bollocks that we unfortunately have to live with in the West of Scotland. The song was never released anywhere else the record label didn't fancy it. It was good though'.

John had some awareness of other fanzines being produced, 'I remember liking *Slow Dazzle* and *Deadbeat*, I also remember Sushil's *Pure Popcorn*

59

and a lot of non-Scottish fanzines that were much more based around what would later be called C86 bands. I don't think I knew anyone else who was producing a fanzine at the time, though, and I think this is important, a lot of the people who helped me or were involved in putting the cassette to varying degrees came from fanzine backgrounds who had gone on to do other things in music – people like Elliot Davis (who was managing Wet Wet Wet and had set up Precious as a record label and management company), Andrea Miller and John Dingwall (who were both writing for the weekly music press by then)'

'So, there was a wider community and the thin boundaries between managers, promoters, fanzine editors, journalists, radio producers and presenters, studio owners (who were often the same people) helped make something like *Honey At The Core* a lot easier to pull together. As well as going to see bands, another way I found out about them was via recording studios and the people that worked there. Within Glasgow, this did not amount to a huge number of people, and it seemed that, although there were the usual petty rivalries, most people were supportive and pulling in the same direction. As a then outsider, I was really surprised at how willing people were to take a chance on me to do this – I had virtually no experience, social skills, or any other credentials, just naïve enthusiasm'.

One man who should probably get more recognition for the Scottish guitar pop explosion of the mid-80s is the man lauded in a display in Tokyo's Wave Record shop as, 'The Godfather of Scottish Pop', Joe McAlinden. At various times a member of The Boy Hairdressers, Groovy Little Numbers, BMX Bandits & Superstar, as well as playing bass on the Soup Dragons' 'Sun Is in The Sky' E.P, and arranging strings on two Teenage Fanclub albums, he's been at the core and centre of all things indie since 1985. Joe reckons that 'fanzines were integral to communicating that freedom to be able to spread our wings. Sushil's zine was great, and I remember our first interview in the Rock Garden in Glasgow with *Coca Cola Cowboy* . It was up there with hearing yourself being played on the radio for the first time'.

For a man so imbued with guitar pop sensibilities, it's interesting to note that his first musical forays were as a member of Motherwell's Youth Orchestra, where he was a classically trained violinist. 'Yeah, I was all set to go to the Royal Scottish Academy of Music, now the Conservatoire, and myself and three people from the Orchestra used to go busking into Glasgow and play Dave Brubeck and Glenn Miller numbers. We began to notice these other lads busking, who would jump on the train at Bellshill and turned out to be Norman Blake, Duglas T Stewart and Sean Dickson'. Along with artist Jim Lambie, they attended the Splash 1 club nights in Glasgow, and from this core of individuals, a whole raft of bands formed, and Joe was absolutely essential to this. A great believer in the DIY ethos and the power of music, it's fitting that 2024 will see the release of a Japanese only compilation featuring Joe's songwriting, with artwork by Jim Lambie. 'I love that fact it's coming out on a physical CD, which incidentally are still massive in Japan, and who knows, it'll maybe get a release in this country too'.

KAW Tapes founder Mark Ritchie found the freedom to communicate how and what you wanted, liberating. 'As a young person in the pre-internet age, zines, tapes and writing letters to people was really important in trying to work out what kind of adult you wanted to become. I once printed a piece that a reader had sent in about why he liked eating meat, even though I totally disagreed with him. I never really saw that counterpoint in the anarcho punk zines. They were more like echo chambers, and I wanted my zines to be like conversations between people who didn't always necessarily agree with each other. I found that more interesting.'

Again, the John Peel show was crucial in the process of not only hearing about fanzines, but also in setting them up. 'I probably first heard about zines on the John Peel show, and one, if not the first, I sent away for was *Kvatch* issue 5, which featured the Housemartins, the Wedding Present, Ivor Cutler and Half Man Half Biscuit, all of whom I was into. The format somehow seemed more accessible than the weekly music papers, more like something I could do myself, and something that I really wanted to do as I'd always been into writing. The zine that followed on from *Kvatch* was *Are You Scared to Get Happy?* and I was fully on board by that point'. Mark's first zine, had the very 'C86-ish' title *Splish! Splash! Splosh!,* and even though he was into the more abrasive stuff like Sonic Youth, the Fall, Stump and the Stupids, that zine was centred around indie/jangle pop. 'I had postal interviews with the Soup Dragons, Shop Assistants, the Clouds, Talulah Gosh, the Sea Urchins, Remember Fun, the Groove Farm, the Rosehips and the Flatmates. I slightly wince at the zine now, but I was only about 15 and the idea that you could write to bands and they'd write back blew my mind. And the music I was writing about seemed like a ray of sunshine compared to all the bland mainstream '80s dross'.

Peel was also crucial to the process of 'regionalization', and the continuing loosening of London's grip as the epicentre of music during the 1980s. Of course, the media ensured that it was dragged right back south with the Britpop nonsense of the mid-1990s, but the die had been cast. 'Even hearing Peel saying "Lanark" was exciting. It made me realise that you could produce zines or music or art from anywhere, which was important in a time when everything seemed to be London based. I'd been to London by then, several times, but it still seemed like a different planet.'

All this musical action wasn't going unnoticed around the cloistered turrets of Portree High School, and in my head I also cooked up an idea of writing a fanzine. However, as I was fumbling with beetled brow in a band on a borrowed bass guitar at the time there was little time to indulge in other musical endeavours. So, the question was, did I become that teenage fanzine writer? No, I didn't. But I suggested one, apparently, to my mate Andy Goddard. Unlike me, he was fired up with journalistic zing, and together with his brother, produced the first music fanzine from the island of Skye. I was keen to probe his mind on the trials and tribulations of running a zine so far from London, or the Central Belt of Scotland, and what issues that threw up, so, I'll let him take up the story.

'As I recall, you rolled the first pebble and suggested we start a fanzine called *Meat Cleaver*. I think we ran with that title for 15 minutes until I rejected it on the grounds of being too Goth. Sometime after that the impetus ran out of steam. But you'd sown the first seed and the idea of making a fanzine wouldn't quite go away. When I pitched it to Simon (his brother and obsessive writer of Bowie books, and the rather fantastic 'Simply Thrilled : The Preposterous Story of Postcard Records') it became a recurring topic of conversation. We'd caught the bug and it was a chance to dig deeper into our love of music and music journalism. From then the zine idea took shape again and *Jingles the Creep* was born'.

'We were only limited by our imagination and in that department there was an unbridled belief – almost arrogance – that the whole world was poised to read our purple prose. Had we grown up in Hammersmith, I doubt we would've had quite the same drive. The comparative isolation of Skye gave us an extra charge: a kind of desperate yearning to connect with the wider popular culture and, by extension, escape. So, no different from a million teenagers growing up, but a rural landscape reminds you of how distanced you are from the things that inspire you. That disconnect lights a fire under your passions – an almost angry kind of energy – and makes you push harder to reach those goals. In that respect, Skye was a help. We may have been less galvanized – more lazy – had we grown up in the city with easier access to record shops and gig venues.

Then again, living on a northerly island was also a hindrance in the unbearable time it took for mail to reach us from London or further afield. This was pre internet and the Royal Mail was the lifeline that linked us to the exciting world of music culture and all things cool. I remember the expectation of seeing the postie's van appear over the hill in Braes and the sinking disappointment when no fanzine mail was delivered'.

Brix Smith Interview, 1986 – Jingles The Creep zine
Courtesy Andy Goddard.

'This was pre internet, so no email or social media. No mobile phones. The Royal Mail was our sine qua non. Sometimes we would use our mum and dad's land-line telephone. I remember phoning Portsmouth punks Red Letter Day and trying to coax them up north to play the Skye Gathering Hall based on little more than thinking it might be a good idea. No money or booking agent or venue liaison. We were just kids buying into the mythology promised by the NME and all our favourite records.

I'm sure if there are teens out there today growing up on Skye, Benbecula or Shetland - with the same insatiable ambition to connect with the world outside - they'll just be a few clicks away from sharing Tweets with someone in Wisconsin or producing a website or digi-zine. Compared to these dotcom whizz kids we were troglodytes armed with sellotape and Sharpie pens. Very analogue. We even used a typewriter to bang out our state-of-the-nation polemic. No PCs or laptops. The smell of Tipp-Ex corrective fluid is a presiding memory from those days'.

I asked Andy if setting up the zine had been partially a reaction against the Ceilidh culture, and the lack of indie action on the island? 'I think you inevitably push against tradition as a teenager. Ceilidh music stood at a polar outpost of the music spectrum I never wanted to visit. Jimmy Shand was hardly Joe Strummer. But I don't recall hating it, I suppose it was never threatening to me in the same way biscuit-factory pop or poodle-perm arena rock – Stock Aitken and Waterman, Bon Jovi etc - dominated the mainstream and subsumed the indie culture. At least, that's how I viewed the state of play through my teen blinkers back in the Eighties. Hilarious in hindsight; a militant indignation that Tiffany had blanket radio approval and Einsturzende Neubauten didn't! But I didn't hate ceilidh culture, I've always found that Brigadoon schtick vaguely comforting. A sort of guilty pleasure'.

'There's a rich history within the indie sphere of artists leaning into the trad and couthie and playing with those juxtapositions - think of Postcard Records or Jessie Rae - and I feel that may have a lot do with its weird appeal. There was always something unavoidably tartan and bagpipey about Big Country. Dunfermline Athletic walk onto the pitch at East End Park to 'Into the Valley' by the Skids and the crowd ebb away post-match to Jimmy Shand's 'Bluebell Polka'. The fact these apparently twee aspects of the culture you're trying to escape are braided into the culture you want to embrace is an endless source of fascination. When you're young you think life is black-and-white and moves in a straight line. You learn over time it's more circular and grey - always shapeshifting - and even the most polarized opposites are somehow connected. I think the truly great artists explore these counterpoints - think of Brian Eno or Damon Albarn – and those that don't are entertainers rather than artists - trading on repetition in a monoculture - like Liam Gallagher'.

The last word on ceilidh? 'I'm now the proud owner of a button accordion – never played – and Jimmy Shand's relentless tour diary would have broken the hardest of metal bands. Never judge a book by its cover'.

If people had heard of the zine, they would have been impressed at the idea of a zine being produced from the a place called Camustianavaig, and would have been surprised at it being a font of indie knowledge in the 1980s. Andy is more sanguine about that now. 'I think most people have never heard of Camustianavaig. John Peel was quite enchanted that a punky indie zine was being produced on the Isle of Skye. I think that was our USP. We just weren't smart enough to monopolize on that. We wanted to be the NME'.

In the last chapter, we looked at the role of cassettes in indie and fanzine culture. School was where we swapped the tapes we'd made up with our pals, and there was a creative craze for designing covers as if they had been released on a 'proper' record label. In their youthful enthusiasm, the lads decided to move it up a notch from our amateur efforts, and set up their own label, Yes Mother Superior.

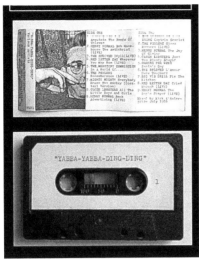

Yabba Yabba Ding Ding –
Courtesy of Andy Goddard.

'We expanded our enterprise... ha ha! We always loved flexi discs and musical giveaways in the music press and the tapes were our crude way of grabbing a piece of this pie. The cassettes became Simon's labour of love. I was always opinionated about the covers and layout and we'd spend long summer days over Fanta and bacon crisps debating the track listing. But the mechanics of making the damn things very much became his pet project.

I think we began 'by 'dubbing' them ourselves or keeping a master copy and doing a tape-to-tape as/when demand came in. We eventually sourced cheap blank cassettes in bulk and would knock up copies and labour over stickers and typeface - again, Simon's patience outranked mine - it became quite monotonous and labour intensive 'mass producing' these compilations even though we hardly broke into the hundreds. Alan Sugar would fire us in a heartbeat. Peelie may have called us 'enterprising' but we never made a dime. Just kids.

The sound quality on the first tape was poor but we improved - thanks to Simon - with further issues of *Jingles*. We even gave away a vinyl 7" on one occasion. A band called The Sun who sounded like a kind of Cure-Lite circa 'Boys Don't Cry' kindly gave us a job lot of sevens to shift. Looking back, maybe they'd split up? But, we were thrilled and felt we now had the chops to take on *ZigZag* and *Melody Maker*'!

'Muriel Gray was tickled by the title of one of our compilation cassettes, 'Dougie Donnelly's Robot Pants,' and gave us a nod in the papers: Glasgow Herald or Daily Record, I can't remember. Would anyone south of the border even know who Dougie Donnelly is - then or now? - and god knows what kind of fever dream threw up that title! Maybe we were playing around with Costello style wordplay or Bowie-ish cut-up techniques? I was

65

incredibly pretentious as a Skye teenager. Peter Easton of Beat Patrol on BBC Radio Scotland was always good to us and would often big up *Jingles* and its accompanying tapes on the Scottish airwaves. He even played our Close Lobsters track. The highlight was John Peel. He marvelled at the Skye connection and called us 'very enterprising'. (For those readers who don't know who Dougie Donelly is, he is a BBC Scotland sports presenter who presented the 'Sportscene' programme of our youth on a Saturday afternoon. Donnelly is known outside Scotland through his involvement in the BBC's networked output of golf, darts, snooker and bowls – so there ya go!)

In terms of the zine sales, it proved difficult to sell from a croft on Skye. 'I could sell you a line and create a myth but, honestly, I doubt we sold more than 40-50 over all three editions. I'm probably being generous too. We sent batches of up to a half-dozen to a Glasgow record store to stock. I can't vouch for the success of sales there but I don't recall retail cheques appearing through our letterbox. The tapes sold better, hardly surprising since we were presenting something tangible - music - rather than adolescent ramblings and lists of our favourite things. It was mostly mail order relying on small ads in the music press and DJ shout-outs on the radio. We expected an endorsement from Peel would boost sales. How wrong we were; kudos far outweighed commerce. Here was another example of Skye being a hindrance, the local avenues of stocking and selling the fanzine were limited - no record shops - salesmanship was never our strong point'

I wondered what Andy thought that the endgame would be for all this. And, bear in mind his youth at this point in time! 'I naively (arrogantly) thought it would set me up for a life as a London rock 'n' roll scribe hanging out with the punk literati. I probably thought I was Skye's answer to Lester Bangs and that *Jingles* would be my entree to a life in the fast lane. I'd soon be propping up a bar in Fitzrovia drinking absinthe with Nick Kent swapping war stories about touring with The Damned. I think perhaps secretly I felt fanzine culture would be some kind of stepping stone towards the Holy Grail of actually joining a band - regardless of my abject laziness and lack of talent in the presence of musical instruments. C'est la vie'.

'John Peel's patronage was definitely the highlight. The Peel show on BBC radio was a mecca for the punk/indie music we loved. Like god giving us a lofty thumbs-up it was the apex of that time. That aside, and with the advantage of age, I can see now the real highlight was the process of actually doing it: the journey. It was a teenage passion that became a hobby-horse and an obsession and, perhaps towards the end, a bit of a chore. It was really just a way of orbiting the things you loved - all that great music - and finding ways to connect to it when you're at that impressionable age. I'm kind of proud we at least did something creative with our time and didn't waste those Skye summers in telly-watching inertia'.

What about the ones that got away? 'The ace in the holes we never interviewed? I guess any member of The Clash. Significantly Joe Strummer who was revered as a demigod back then. Strange to think his granny came from Raasay within view of Camustianavaig. Again, those curveball connections you don't expect. Who else? Adam Ant would've been a coup for me. I was always a closet pirate! And John Lydon was, and is always good interview value for shits and giggles'

Around this time, our circle of friends had become aware of Scottish bands, via the likes of the C86 cassette, and in many ways it was the age of a real outpouring of Scottish Indie music (Close Lobsters/Primal Scream/Shop Assistants etc). I wondered if Andy had consciously tried to tap into that. 'Yes, definitely. Though I nurtured a love-hate thing with the Scottish scene - biting the hand that feeds! - I loved the more abrasive sound of the Shop Assistants but the early Scream were lost on me and I loathed the tweeness of Strawberry Switchblade, et al. But the buzz about Scotland and Scottish bands at that time definitely gave us a push and a sense of entitlement to crank a fanzine out into the world'.

Andy and I have discussed how in a weird way the Dunvegan boys penchant for sugary-fuzz driven bands, and the Camustianavaig boys liking for Beefheart-damaged bands reflected the similar West/East coast divide of Glasgow and Edinburgh. Strange but true! 'We gave column inches to The Big Gun from Irvine whose single 'Heard About Love' is one of the great underrated Scottish indie gems of the Eighties'. The Big Gun featured one Andrew O'Hagan on tambourine. Andrew of course, went onto to become one the UK's finest writers, but always retained his fiery Scottishness. In a contemporary review *Smash Hits* magazine said the track 'was the kind of single that made England great'. O'Hagan wrote in immediately, of course: 'Dear Smash Hits, we come from Scotland, so fuck you!'

'The Tremens from Glasgow also graced our pages with their auld Scots lunatic asylum punk'. The Tremens, or The Glasgow Tremens, as they were later called, were a band buried far too deeply in the undergrowth for any record labels to bother with, but main man Raymy Travers acknowledges their deathless classics 'Here Come The Plods' and the boozy 'Shake Prattle And Fall', which were included 'on a now very hard-to-find compilation called Dougie Donnelly's Robot Pants which changes hands for silly money these days'. Andy also managed to get Paisley's Close Lobsters on the lads' 'Yabba Yabba Ding Ding' compilation, and notes that 'I see they've reformed as well. Again, the circle of life. The past catches up with you in ways you don't expect'.

Andrew Burnett of the Close Lobsters calls it 'Brilliant stuff. Great that John Peel played it too' and adds that 'that Bob Stanley bloke out of St Etienne put that demo out on a record from his fanzine *The Caff Corporation*. We put him up and took him to see Partick Thistle when he came up from London. Now he's famous he seems to have forgotten about The Lobsters sadly'.

Chapter 6 :

Toothpaste Traces – Women's New Directions

Other Glamour... editors unknown.

One of the lesser known socio-political movements to emerge from punk that played a major role in putting anti-sexism on the agenda was Rock Against Sexism (RAS). RAS, galvanised by the success of Rock Against Racism, formed in 1979 to tackle the misogyny that women faced in both the music business, and in society in general. RAS contributors emphasised collective action and intersectional feminism. One of RAS's most significant voices was Lucy Toothpaste (Lucy Whitman), who not only wrote extensively for the RAR fanzine, *Temporary Hoarding*, but co-edited and wrote for the official RAS fanzine, *Drastic Measures*. Before this, she had founded her own feminist zine, *Jolt*. *Jolt* ran for three issues, and as Jon Savage noted in his fanzine round up in Sounds in early 1978, it was one of the few early fanzines to use the medium's lack of censorship to express a political opinion.

Prior to *Jolt*, in the autumn of 1976, Lucy had formed a performance band, The Neons, with some friends. The band was influenced as much by Dada and Surrealism as by what was going on in the world of punk. "It was six women," she explains, "and we did four performances, and then our beautiful neon sign flew off the top of the car and smashed, and the band broke up!" Lucy's activities highlighted the central role that punk played for many women in developing a feminist consciousness, and contributed to a train of thought which reverberated through to the riot grrrl movement of the '90s.

In general however, the role of women in punk zines in the 1970s is largely unacknowledged. Lucy admits that there were hardly any other writers around, even in the London area 'There was Vinyl Virgin and Crystal Clear, who did *More On*, and then there was my friend Sharon, who called herself Sharon Spike, and she did *Apathy In Ilford*, and that's about it, that I was aware of anyway – not saying there weren't any others, but they were the ones I knew about.' In Scotland there were few women directly involved in the punk and post punk scenes. Honourable exceptions go to Fay Fife of the Rezillos and Hilary Morrison of The Flowers, the person jointly responsible for setting up the Fast Product label in Edinburgh. On being the front person of a punk/new wave band, Fay recalls 'different times - I remember being referred to as 'the chick singer' once or twice. There were one or two ladies singing at that time, but more in soul influenced bands - not a lot of 'em! I don't think I noticed I was a woman in the early days all that much. I was a green horn though - I didn't always act in my own best interests. There were subtle prejudices - it was always assumed for example that 'sound' & the general recording was the proclivity of the non-females - on occasion some folk treated me like a cherry on a tree but mostly I was too busy to notice and I just got on with it'

Lindsay Hutton acknowledges the lasting influence of the Slits in pointing a way forward, 'I never got The Slits at the time but one thing they did do was allow girls to have a go so, from that point alone, they're far more important than much of your first wave of punks. I think there were always women that just did their own thing, but the dominant male bullshit persisted for sure. I think that girls maybe had a bigger hand in developing DIY and taking other routes rather than sporting what was perceived to be technical ability in the conventional sense'.

The Slits had created a new template for women in rock bands, at a complete remove from what had gone on before. Still active when The Slits were forming, the American glam/hard rock band, The Runaways, were put together and kept under tight control by their coercive and domineering manager, Kim Fowley. The Slits smartly managed to avoid a relationship with the similarly inclined Malcolm McLaren, and set themselves free to do whatever they wanted. And they did. 'We saw ourselves as role models' says drummer Paloma, 'although we didn't want anybody putting a label on us, we stood for girls as much as we stood for not wanting to live by anybody's rules. The song FM, which I wrote, has the line *today's transmission will give me the solution,* and that's obviously not the case'.

Slits Scrapbook - Jolt Fanzine Reviews
Courtesy Of Paloma Romero McLardy.

Jill Bryson, later of Glasgow band Strawberry Switchblade was motivated by the creative opportunities afforded by the era, and bands like The Slits. 'I vividly remember being extremely excited about starting Art School. I had been involved with the punk scene in Glasgow since '77 so I was used to hanging about with creative people. Initially, I was disappointed with Art School as the students seemed a bit pedestrian compared to my friend group, but I loved the place and found it endlessly stimulating. The Victoria cafe sometimes had bands playing at lunchtime but the venue I remember was at the Haldane Building, which was an ex-Police Horse stables turned Art studios. I saw Orange Juice and Simple Minds (amongst others) play in the large Hall which had huge repeat screen prints of 60's model Jean Shrimpton at the back of the stage. Non students could get in so it was good varied audience'.

And the scene which coalesced around Orange Juice provided opportunities to get involved. 'My boyfriend at the time (Peter McArthur) was a photography student who documented the punk scene and took photos of the bands. Edwyn Collins and David McClymont studied graphics at the same college as him and they became friends. Orange Juice were a real anomaly in the post punk scene in Glasgow at the time. Most bands were pursuing a more electronic dystopian vibe and Orange Juice looked like 1950's Boy Scouts and played jangly guitar music. It was inspiring and they were totally into everyone around them having a go themselves. It was great to be around when Postcard records was getting off the ground - so much DIY creativity all around. I remember colouring in record covers and printing t-shirts and fanzines at the Glasgow print studios'. Her musical partner, Rose McDowall had started off as a 'standyuppy' drummer, al la Moe Tucker, in a band called The Poems, 'we were kind of punky, but kind of moving on beyond punk, if you know what I mean'. It's interesting to note that the standing up, basic drumming approach was adopted by several Scottish bands like the JAMC and the Shop Assistants, but Rose got there first – certainly in this country!

The post-punk scene during and after the demise of Postcard records, and a less macho attitude towards women seem to afford more opportunities. Female or mixed gender bands in the '80s proliferated – Strawberry Switchblade, Altered Images, the Ettes, The Vultures, Fakes, Metropak, Shop Assistants, Jesse Garon & The Desperadoes, Baby Lemonade, The Twinsets, Pastels, The Fizzbombs and Delmontes to name a few. The Delmontes from Edinburgh released just two excellent singles in 1980 and 1981, and split at the start of 1983. Boasting an avant-futurist retro sound, and comprising a male/female line up, one of whom, Bernice Simpson drummed with the Pastels for seven years afterwards. 'She's a really good drummer' opined Stephen Pastel to *Slow Dazzle* in 1984, adding gleefully that 'if we have trouble with anyone we just send Bernice round to kick their face in!'.....Now he's a little more circumspect with his language, but the sentiment is still positive. And on the gender make-up of the band, as he says 'it was never part of a plan, but we were always just open to having the right people. Working with Annabel (1984-2000) and Katrina (1989-Present) has been extremely positive. It's made the band more three-dimensional in a way. The three of us spent a lot of time together and that has helped immensely'.

On being in a mixed gender band on the Scottish circuit in the 1980s, Bernice had this to say in Melody Maker in 1982, 'When we first started, it was all 'Ha ha - ridiculous! How can you have a female drummer?' Singer Julie Hepburn noted to *Other Glamour* fanzine that 'The Delmontes are not a band of three girls and two boys, but of people chosen for their abilities, and because of their friendship'. In the same issue, Flowers singer and guitarist Hilary Morrison is clear that 'we enjoy fun, action, good times, whatever....and society's present set of rules about male/female we think are pretty limiting, dismally boring and extremely repetitive'.

Jill Bryson agrees with that summary, 'The punk and post punk scene as well as the Art School scene was not typical of Glasgow at the time. Most people were pretty hostile to us and the media took no notice until we got interest from big companies. Some people within the industry were dismissive of women in bands. I wouldn't say we were taken seriously. Most of our songs dealt with darker issues but our image was the thing that most people wanted to talk about. I like to think our image was a bit dark and weird but trivialising it kind of mitigated us. Reduced us to impotent 'girlies' instead of strong women with something to say. To be honest, the record label was constantly trying to rub off our rough edges and it didn't feel good'.

On the formation of the Shop Assistants into the four fifths female line up up who recorded the classic 'Safety Net' E.P, guitarist David Keegan recalls, 'apart from very much wanting the band to have a woman singer, it all happened organically – Sarah (bass) was on the same course as me at Napier College in Edinburgh, and she joined in late 1984. Then for the first few gigs we had a guy called Craig drumming. Sarah recruited Ann on drums and then Laura joined in time for recording the first EP – there wasn't a plan to have two drummers, it just happened! My line at the time was that it made no difference whether the members were men or women (apart from the singer's voice) but in retrospect it really did matter – both from the way we sounded and inspiring other women to be in bands and make records'.

Many of the woman in bands brought a different and unique expressive and artistic intent into their bands, such as Edinburgh noise merchants, The Vultures. Speaking to Cloudberry Records blog, vocalist Janie Nicoll explained the bands origins. 'They were myself, Allison Young on bass, Anna Watkins onlead guitar and Ian Binns on Drums. Anna, Allison and I were all at Edinburgh College of Art in the same year. Allison and I were in the Tapestry Department, which was and still is, a very forward thinking department, more about installation than weaving. Then I changed to Painting. We both had a fairly punky approach to our work. Allison used make up the posters, just collaging images together in quite a spontaneous jokey way, that worked really well, and she also designed the cover for the EP, so it was influenced by that sixties Psychedelic look, but in quite a tongue in cheek kind of a way. Very rough and ready, but we were all into the sixties garage sound of the Sonics'.

It was a small, but vibrant scene in Edinburgh from the second half of the decade, with band members moonlighting in other bands, in common with the later Glasgow scene.' Allison and Anna, had persuaded Ian to be the drummer and a bit later asked me to join the band, and we started practicing in the practice rooms off Blair Street, sharing with Jesse Garon & The Deperadoes and Rote Kapelle and various other bands. We didn't have a drum kit, amps or any equipment so we used the other bands' equipment.' The band went on to produce one fine EP, and recorded a BBC Radio 1 session for Janice Long.

If there is an East Coast, and female, equivalent of Joe McAlinden, then surely that honour must go to Margarita Vasquez Ponte. At various times a member of Rote Kapelle, Jesse Garon, The Fizzbombs and The Shop Assistants, in the guise of drummer, guitarist and vocalist, as she admits there was no big plan in all this, 'just people asking people they liked, their pals if they wanted to be in a band...fully organic I would say'.

Growing up in the Highlands and rural Aberdeenshire, a child of Spanish parents, she also found herself at Napier College in 1984, along with a whole host of other students who would go on to form the backbone of Edinburgh's independent music scene. She found herself in the middle of a shifting, mutually supportive scene where mixed gender bands seemed to be the norm, rather than the exception. 'To be honest, at the time it never even occurred to me that I would not be able to do anything I wanted to. I never felt like a girl in a band, I just felt like I was in a band with my pals and it did not matter if it was a male or female mix, we were just people making music.'

'I have to say I was very lucky, there was no otherness about being female coming from anyone in my circle, we just got on with it. I did not feel I needed any support or kinship form other women as I just assumed they would be there too on the scene in the same way I was'. However, she adds that, 'my naiveté had protected me as I just blithely got on with doing my own thing my own way. I realised how important feminism was, and how women should and needed to support each other and I that i was living my life as a feminist; I just had not put a name or a label on it'.

'The bands kind of developed one from the other, so for quite a long time they were all going simultaneously. What can I say? That was our entertainment...the more bands you were in, the more gigs and touring and hopefully records and sessions you would get'. Finding herself in several different bands necessitated the shifting of roles and instruments, and she found herself behind the drumkit for her first band Rote Kapelle. 'I loved, and still love Mo Tucker. Bernice Simpson was hugely inspiring, especially as The Pastels played my friend's birthday party, and I thought Bernice was so cool, such a great drummer, nothing flashy, just a great beat'. She also drummed for a reactivated Shop Assistants in 1989, as part of a short lived final line up. 'Well Alex had left kind of suddenly and the

74

Shop Assistants still wanted to go on. I had been on most of their tours with them, mostly just as a pal, but occasionally I had filled in on drums and also the Desperadoes supported them a lot. I was the logical person to take on the drums for this last hurrah... did say that I would be using the full kit rather than the paired down 2 drum set up they had had before and that would change the sound a bit. Also, I couldn't drum as fast on the full kit!

In between times, she formed The Fizzbombs with Jesse Garon drummer Angus McPake, with Margarita moving to guitar. Completing this rotating cast was singer Katy Lironi, and Ann Donald, who had played drums with the Shop Assistants – now installed on bass guitar! 'Basically, the Desperadoes liked to do Blondie covers in our set, and usually Angus would move to the drums and I would play guitar and put some harmonies on Fran's vocals. We both enjoyed this shift in roles so we decided to form the Fizzbombs so we could do more of that. It was really just for our entertainment, we were not thinking we would put a record out or anything, just play a few gigs, that sort of thing!! I was by no means a great musician, but I enjoyed everything'

Fizzbombs – Image courtesy Douglas MacIntyre.

Learning together as a gang certainly seemed to be half the fun for her bandmate Katy Lirioni, and the gender seemed unimportant. 'To be honest we were so young I don't think, certainly for myself, I gave it that much thought. It all seemed so normal, we were just people in a band, the fact we were boys or girls didn't seem that important. It was more that we were all learning together. For me it was important that it was all about a spirit

75

of innovation and there wasn't any massively knowledgeable musician, male or female in the band'.

The small and incestuous nature of the Edinburgh scene helped them get signed to Eddie Connelly's Narodnik Records. Eddie had been a member of Meat Whiplash, one of Creation Records' earliest signings, and in 1987 became The Motorcycle boy when departing Shoppies singer joined them. 'At that time, Eddie was going out with Alex from the Shop Assistants (Alex had been in Rote Kapelle before me and left to devote all her time to the Shop Assistants). As we were all friends and part of the same Edinburgh scene, Eddie came with Alex to some of our gigs, he told us he wanted to put our record out and that was that, we were delighted! Same thing happened with the Fizzbombs, we had barely formed and again he offered to put out a record on Narodnik, again, we were delighted, Angus and I had formed the band just for fun and to play some different instruments!'

In Edinburgh, The Twinsets formed by Rachel and Gaye Bell combined their own love of 60s girl groups, like the Shangri-Las, but with the added attitude, and swagger of punk. They did at least one John Peel session, and self released a cassette only single 'Heartbeat' in 1983.

Sophisticated Boom Boom were an all female band, this time from Glasgow, who mutated into the poppier, His Latest Flame. As agit-popsters Sophisticated Boom Boom, they recorded a John Peel session, but never graduated to vinyl. A name change and a contract with Go! Discs failed to rouse the record buying public, despite some fine pop tunes, leaving them in the unenviable position of being patronized as an "all-girl group" by some and pilloried by others in the media for growing out of their monkey-booted adolescence. Perhaps they were the nearest Scotland ever got to producing an all-girl pop band akin to The Bangles, but it was not to be, and they called it a day in 1990.

However, attitudes from the media were shifting in some measure as Jill Bryson explains. 'When we had our hit with Since Yesterday, (it reached number 5 in the UK Singles Charts) I would say local media and bands were very supportive. We did our share of fanzine interviews, some of which didn't see the light of day but were fun to do. That was 1985 and attitudes had changed a lot. There were a few colourful characters around in the charts so we weren't quite as out on a limb as before. I really hope we inspired women to get into music. Punk spawned many strong female characters that influenced me for sure so I can only hope to be a wee part of that'.

The Vaselines formed a couple of years later in Glasgow, a duo comprising Eugene Kelly and Frances McKee, famously becoming Kurt Cobain's favourite band. Frances Mckee's experience was different to Jill Bryson's in that she felt that she didn't experience any prejudice at all, and any issues came from being a 'non musician'. 'I don't think it was a case of gaining acceptance. We just did what we did, again the insecurities came from just learning to play guitar. I definitely did not want to be 'the girl in the band'. Eugene and I wanted it to look equal and I learned to play guitar because of that. This made our sound, as I could only play a few chords'.

Into this prevailing attitude, a number of women fanzine writers entered the fray. Jill Bryson remembers that 'There were plenty of fanzines around. James Kirk (Orange Juice) and Peter worked on one – to be called *Strawberry Switchblade*, which never saw the light of day. Edwyn interviewed Viv Albertine of the Slits for that – Peter took photos. I remember one of the articles was a tongue in cheek tutorial on how to fail a dead end job interview. I remember being involved in a fanzine with Stephen Pastel and Peter called *Juniper Beri Beri*. It was a real 'just do it' time. If you had an idea, you ran with it.

Juniper Beri-Beri Courtesy Stephen Pastel.

Stephen Pastel admits that when his band first started, the support for their music was probably the fanzines, which were more important for them than the NME or more mainstream press, although they did have supporters like Paul Morley and Dave McCullough. In terms of *Juniper Beri Beri* Stephen admits that it was a bit of a knockabout effort, 'and I think that there were maybe other fanzines at the time that maybe had better writing, but it was nice to be a part of that community. It was an exciting community.' It also, seemingly, inspired other budding musicians to get involved. 'David Keegan saw the zine and felt that he was a fellow traveller.' And that linked across to Stephen's friend Annabel Wright, better known as Aggi, later to join Buba and The Shop Assistants, and eventually, The Pastels themselves, as their bass player. Annabel was one of the main people behind *Juniper Beri Beri*. 'Although we were political people', says Stephen, 'the zines weren't political in themselves. They were really quite spontaneous. Annabel and I had a sense of the possibilities available at that time, and I think that is maybe why *Juniper Beri Beri* is more...amateur. When Jon (Smale) and Robina came on board for *Pastelism*, they were probably a bit more thorough'. Jon, who later went on to become a historian contributed to the first issue of *Pastelism* in 1988 that features an interview with Teenage Fanclub, a substantial article on Daniel Johnston, and a pen portrait of Jon as a member of *Pastelism's* 'one big happy family' that carries a self-description as having 'the looks of his dad and the brains of his ma – unlucky as fuck!'

Margarita Vasquez Ponte remembers this era of zine production fondly. 'I loved fanzines - we all did. I think they were the real storytellers for our music scene, more so than the music press in the mid 80's at least. Wherever we played, I would buy a local one, and I would pick them up at gigs, I still have a big collection of them. Randomly I would mention *Coca Cola Cowboy*, *Juniper Beri Beri*. *S*uper DIY! You get first interviews of bands who later became huge, they are treasures!

And two other Fizzbombs, Katy and Ann, later put together their own zine *The Erotic Urges of Creeping Bent*. 'Ann and I have always written and been involved in music. Ann was a journalist and I was involved in creative writing... we'd both just finished our post grad in English studies and liked he whole cut up thing, found poetry, the guerrilla girls etc. It was just a bit of fun'

....

Moving forward into the 1990's, Amanada Mackinnon from Glasgow band bis (known as Manda Rin) was involved with several fanzines such as *Paper Bullets*, *Funky Spunk* and *Popgirl*. She acknowledges the importance of fanzines in the spread of information. 'If it wasn't for fanzines, our first single wouldn't have happened. It was guitarist Steven's zine that the owner of Acuerela Records in Spain bought whilst visiting Glasgow and got in touch to release our first 7" Transmissions on the Teen-c Tip'.

Funky Spunk & Paper Bullets Joint Issue Courtesy of Manda Rin.

On a more basic level, Manda felt that zines were a fantastic way of hearing about new things happening musically, and wanted to be part of that communication chain. 'We were big fans of fanzines in the early/mid 90's in particular as it was sometimes the only way to discover new and sometimes teeny bands all around the world. Mainstream media didn't cover that many of these and it was pre-internet, Bandcamp and Spotify so I felt an urge to let people know about bands I'd discovered. I also like the personal and sometimes unprofessional way of writing, so I just thought why the hell not, and started one myself. Steven did *Paper Bullets* and my first one was *Funky Spunk*. That was a tiny 1p zine as I was nervous starting out, but I even got written interviews with the Beastie Boys and Sleeper for it! I later did *Popgirls* and interviewed so many amazing women in bands like Sleater-Kinney and the Donnas about tiny underground independent bands that I wouldn't have heard otherwise.' And in terms of her favourites? 'Apart from your own *Hype!* of course, I liked Urusei Yatsura's *Kitten Frenzy* and our soon-to-be long-term friend Dee's zine called *All About D & Friends'*.

Elaine Graham – Image courtesy Graham Kemp.

Self proclaimed 'geek rockers', Urusei Yatsura from Glasgow featured Elaine Graham on bass. On the formation of the band, guitarist Graham Kemp has this to say, 'We were very keen to not just be another band of four lads. Very boring. It was really pure coincidence though. Fergus met Elaine by chance and really liked her. She played guitar so he essentially dared her to play bass for the band we were trying to put together. She was in because she was good at it'. Uresei Yatsura were keen DIY enthusiasts, and set up their own zine, *Kitten Frenzy.* Another Glasgow band from this period, The Delgados, who featured Emma Pollock on guitar, went on to set up their own seminal 'Chemikal Undergound' label which later featured the likes of Arab Strap and Mogwai. All female bands around at the time included the original line up of Lung Leg, and the semi-legendary garage punkers, Pink Kross who released their 'Chopper Chix from V.P Hell' album on bis' own Teen-C Records label.

Pink Kross - courtesy Graham Kemp.

Although Manda feels that there have been steps in the right direction, there is still a distance for women to travel before they are able to get an equal footing in the music business. 'I think there's more awareness of this issue, but I'm not convinced that things have improved massively for women in being taken more seriously in general. My 10-year-old son is a fan of some female stars like Taylor Swift and Lady Gaga who write and perform their own music so he doesn't see or feel the hardship that I often talk about. We just need more women being out there doing it to help change the minds of future generations and I'm now seeing with my son that this definitely helps and that women aren't just a token or rarity in learning an instrument'.

Other female edited zines proliferated during the Nineties. Titles such as *Boa, Jelly Bean Machine, Fluid, GroundLeft & Cute Kids on Medication* were all produced north of the border. In contrast to the female edited zines of the 1980s, which were mainly music focussed, these zines brought womens' issues to the fore, mingling cartoons, dark humour, music reviews and an exhortation to 'just do it'. Saskia Holling of Edinburgh garage rockers, The Nettelles remembers 'the other fanzines produced by members of other Glasgow and Edinburgh bands that I often played on the same bill with. Namely, *Bittersweet* by Maureen from Lung Leg, *Violet* by Lucy McKenzie of Batfink and Ganger, *Charity Shopper* by Katrina Dixon of Policecat, and later Sally Skull'.

For Saskia, growing up in the Outer Hebridean island of Lewis, meant experiencing her music in a similar way to myself, and many other youngsters who grew up on the islands at the time. 'I actually bought my first vinyl when I went to Oban with the Stornoway Primary School Gaelic choir to sing in the 1978 Mod - a mòd being an Eisteddfod-inspired festival of Scottish Gaelic song, arts and culture. I can't remember what record shop I went to but I bought two singles; Rose Royce 'Love Don't Live Here Anymore' and Stevie Wonder 'I Wish' – I was 10 and had seen these performed on Top Of The Pops and wanted them!'. Being so far away from any sort of metropolitan youth culture meant finding your way through the music maze. 'I was a teenager on the island from '81 to mid '85 and was pretty open to any kind of music. I would dance at school discos with my 'alternative' friends to the 'alternative' chart stuff like Teardrop Explodes, Strawberry Switchblade, Adam Ant and even a bit of Human League. But I was also into heavy metal for a while because I think everyone on the islands goes through that phase! I had been introduced to punk when I was 13 or 14 by a group of friends, some of whom had played on 'Sad Day We Left The Croft' but I could never really believe that people I knew had played on a record that had been released and played on the radio – it just seemed to be too farfetched'.

A lack of an alternative music scene, and access to even fewer musical role models than on the mainland, meant that Saskia didn't entertain the idea of being in a band or becoming involved with any underground writing, and it wasn't until a few years later, and a move to Edinburgh that she started to formulate ideas of putting her thoughts onto paper. 'I knew Aggi of The Pastels had created *Juniper Beri Beri* because one of the bands I had come across with people that influenced a more 'do it' thought pattern in me was The Pastels. I was also aware of Lindsay Hutton's *Next Big Thing* although I didn't come across that until the early '90s. I did buy a lot of comics though! Apart from the Hernandez brothers' *Love and Rockets*, I mostly bought female penned comics – Mary Fleener, Dame Darcy, Roberta Gregory and, of course, Julie Doucet who did a comic called *Dirty Plotte*. But the biggest inspiration for me was Riot Grrrl. 'In March 1993 I went to a Huggy Bear and Bikini Kill gig at The Cathouse in Glasgow. In addition to the inspiration to make a musical noise, the place was full of fanzines. I had been keeping a diary for years and for some time my diaries had been full of political rants as well as notes on things that happened in my day – reading the fanzines bought at this gig, I realised that I could be putting my political thoughts out there in a fanzine.'

By April 1993 she was rehearsing with a band called Fudd and played her first gig by the end of May. In October that year, the band played a gig in Demarcos in Edinburgh where she launched her zine. 'It was for this gig that I made my first *Heavy Flow* – a feminist fanzine talking about period poverty (before it was ever a 'thing') and calling for free period products but advocating that people steal them in the meantime!' She remembers it as a very supportive time 'Selling each other's zines at gigs and encouraging each other to do more. Pat Laureate of Melody Dog and later Vesuvius Records was also very supportive of everybody and indeed, Vesuvius put out their own zine *Off The Road* with an accompanying cassette in 1996'. That cassette was 'A Fistful of Horsepower', and featured, amongst others, The Pastels, Jad Fair, Lungleg & Ganger 'There were other observations in the zine too, questions around gender stereotypes and about women's representation in music mags'.

Heavy Flow Courtesy of Saskia Holling.

As I produced more issues (there were six in total) to be sold at more all-ages gigs that I organised, there was less ranting and more music and also more contributions from other people. So, there were interviews with various music people, gig and record reviews, fictional stories and still a few thoughts and rants!' And most importantly, her initial reason for the fanzine, calling for free period products, has now been answered by the 2021 (Free) Period Products Act in Scotland.

Some zines were started for less lofty reasons. Mhairi McClymont started her zine *Muzzle*, with her school pals in Johnstone, simply as a means to get into gigs. 'Hole were playing in Glasgow, and we'd heard that if you had a fanzine going, you could get in for free'. Being very young, and being outside the Glasgow indie scene, writing a zine was a way to connect in and be part of a connection to music. Nobody was covering the developing nu-metal scene at the time, and the girls set about trying t put that right. 'We interviewed Korn, Deftones, Incubus and also the likes of Green Day. But we also had comedy skits about Neds, so we couldn't sell it at school'. As a bit of explanation for any non-Scottish reader, a Ned is a young troublemaker with a taste for tonic wine, dodging train fares, vandalism and generally hates alternative culture!

When Mhairi finished school and went on to university, she stopped producing *Muzzle*. 'Nu-metal had gone downhill, and people like Fred Durst had ruined in with his frat-boy rubbish'. She wanted to produce a zine that was more self consciously political, and started up *No, I'm a Veronica* with friends in 2000. The zine covered topics such as contraception, race & identity politics, and ran for three issues until she got, as she says, 'her first proper job with the BBC'.

Scottish reviewer for Melody Maker in the early '90s was Lucy Sweet, and that came about almost by accident. 'I went in for a competition to win the best 50 albums of 1992 and you had to write a review - I really wanted the records, so I wrote two. (I think maybe I reviewed Babes in Toyland, but I can't remember the other one.) I had no idea that it was their secret way of recruiting new reviewers. But I got a call from the reviews ed Jim Arundel (now writing under his own name - Jim Irvin) saying I hadn't won but I was the only person who sent in two reviews, so would I write for them?' Women in the 1970's had recounted some appallingly sexist and misogynistic behaviour from their male colleagues, but it did seem to have improved somewhat in the interim. Lucy recalls that she 'only went (in to the office) once - I still have my IPC visitor pass somewhere... it was so weird because you came out of the lift and in one direction there was the NME office and the other was Melody Maker. That blew my mind'.

'The office was mostly men but people like Julie Burchill had broken new ground for female writers and Caitlin Moran was getting her start there at the same time. There was also the lovely Sara Manning and a writer called Victoria Segal who was really good. I can't speak for their experiences, but at the time it felt like women were breaking through and making our voices heard, and we were giving as good as we got. Jim was great to me- very encouraging and kind, and he made sure female-fronted bands got coverage.' She recalls it as a fun time, where I was mostly known for slagging people off. (I think I thought I was Steven

Wells or something and hey, it was the 90s - everybody was doing it) Someone once wrote into the letters page with the question 'Who the f*** does Lucy Sweet think she is?' Today that would have probably been a tweet.'

At the same time she was posting her reviews for MM, she was getting into the fanzine scene. 'My fanzine days started in Newcastle, inspired I think by Rachel Holborow's *Slampt* zines, which were works of art. They were feminist Riot Grrrl zines and pulled no punches. There was a crossover with comic books and music zines, and I got more into comics at that time - specifically Daniel Clowes' *Eightball* and *Hate* by Peter Bagge.' She went to Seattle in 1993, and returned inspired by the riot grrrl movement and Julie Doucet's comic book Dirty Plotte, to set up her own 'feminist body positive comic in reaction to the 90s heroin chic trend', called *Unskinny*. 'it also had a comic strip called The Craps about the crap grunge bands I'd been seeing, who all had long hair and looked like they were called Steve. I sold it through Forbidden Planet and it built up a decent following.' It also led to an unexpected lifetime romantic attachment for Lucy. 'John Peel once devoted a good 15 mins of his show to it in 1994 and a boy working in the Paisley branch of Food Giant heard it and wrote to me. We started the most 90s mixtape and letter correspondence ever, and in '95 I moved to Glasgow to live with him. We've been married 26 years now'!

The move to Glasgow proved to be fruitful from a musical point of view as well. 'The zine culture in Glasgow was thriving at that point. My friend Kirsty Dalziel did one called *GroundLeft* which was about the hardcore scene, and Amanda from Bis was the zine queen at that time - also Lucy McKenzie who is now an artist. We also used to love *Ben Is Dead*, an American music zine which we picked up at Tower Records'.

'I loved Bikini Kill and Hole and Royal Trux, and of course there were so many bands in Glasgow like Bis and Lungleg that just seemed to be having the most fun'. Bikini Kill's Kathleen Hanna was a focal point for many female writers. Glasgow comic artist Heather Middleton interviewed Hanna and her follow up band, Le Tigre in Glasgow, and found it both refreshing and liberating compared with an awkward encounter with a male band manager. 'I wrote asking if I could interview them on behalf of Glasgow Women's Library as I hadn't started making my own zines at that stage. We squeezed into a tiny backstage cupboard and I was wired with nerves but they could not have been more delightful, focused and fascinating, and also interested in me. I was quite naive, asking something about their tour bus like they were Pearl Jam - they ruefully told me they were squeezed into a tour "vanigan" as they called it, still getting changed in toilets etc. It felt like they were invested in co-creating a good experience with me, like older punk sisters'.

Le Tigre cartoon by Heather Middleton.

Manda Rin cites both Bikini Kill and The Slits as an influence on her having the confidence to get involved. 'I was probably quite politically naïve at just 16, but understood a good portion of the situations these bands sang about and it certainly opened me up to many issues I wouldn't have been aware of otherwise. I didn't have a lot of confidence so to see unconventional looking women jumping around onstage and singing in an aggressive and shouty manner was so empowering looking. Once again, I thought 'why the hell not'? I couldn't play an instrument professionally, I had a tiny, quiet voice and was quite shy but I was also influenced being around John and Steven (bis band members) who were a similar age and making music, albeit doing it VERY well.

Lucy Sweet reckons 'It was a liberating time because so many women were starting their own bands. The prevailing attitude was 'well, how hard can it be?' Of course, the sound guy would be patronising, or the guy at the guitar shop would be a dick, but there was a determination and a momentum that was really refreshing. I think that had as much to do with the DIY ethic as feminism itself – it felt like the possibilities were endless because we were in charge of our own creative output. It was raw, ramshackle and unedited, but it belonged to us'.

Chapter 7 :

Big Noises & Beat Rhythm News in the 'Sneck

Sometime in the early 1990's I had a strange inkling to become a journalist, and specifically a music journalist, despite having had no previous desire to write about music, nor experience. I'd never paid that much attention to the bozos who hacked it out for NME, Sounds or Melody Maker. In fact, I'd preferred the glossier offerings of Record Mirror and Smash Hits as a youngster, and also the style bible, The Face, when I progressed through my teens. Growing up in Skye, a ferry journey and 100 miles or more from the nearest record shop, you were limited back in the '80s as to what music journals you could lay your sweaty hands on, so sometimes you just read what was available. Having said that, the music journalists of the 'inkies' always seemed like old bores who couldn't just enjoy music without applying a bit of Barthes or Gramsci to give the impression of their intrinsic and great intellectualism. And so Stalinist as well. My esteemed friend Andy, recently admitted to me that he stopped listening to The Police because Steven Wells, aka 'Swells', had instructed him to do so from the pages of the NME. Well, maybe not instructed him exactly, but his copy of 'Regatta De Blanc' soon quietly found its way to the back of his record collection. C'est la vie.

With my first scribblings being committed to print in the local newspaper by dint of it being a very slow news week, I began to wonder if I could turn this writing lark into some sort of semi-permanent gig. The answer to that in the long run was in the negative, but I decided to have a go anyway.

So, it was on the blower to Andy, and across several conversations, the seeds of *Hype*! began fermenting in our heads. I wanted to document the club scene in the Highlands, and yes, there was one, and it was actually quite good. By 1993 I was bored with indie-guitar music, and a zine which covered the Highlands and beyond with free tapes on the cover seemed like something I had to do. Andy, always a brilliant cartoonist, hatched the concept of 'Mad Crofter DJ', a boiler suited smallholder-cum-clubber-cum-DJ from Nairn with his posse The 3 Murdos 3 - who caused chaos wherever they went - and all of a sudden, we were up and running.

One of the nice things to come out of this swirling stew of ideas was our adoption by Adam Sutherland at Highland Printmakers in Inverness. Adam was the tweedy, louche and laid back director of said studio and gallery. I think I went in one day and explained the idea for the zine, and his reaction was, 'sure, come in and use the place as a base'. He seemed to view us with wry amusement flavoured with some genuine affection. 'The Sound of

Young-ish Inverness' he dubbed us, which I liked. I also liked his admiration for London punks 999's shoes. They were the only punk band worth watching in '77, he boldly asserted. 'Always very colourful and expensive' he noted admiringly, as if it was quite simply the only reason to like a particular group. He loftily claimed to have been in a band with Pete Astor of the Loft and Weather Prophets fame, but I never could find a shred of evidence for this claim. We did however try, along with one of the gallery assistants, to form a keyboard/drums only garage rock outfit with Adam bashing on the skins. His affectation of wearing a tweed cloak would have looked great behind the drum stool, although he seemed to have endured some abuse from Inverness van drivers when barrelling through the town on his bike, with said cloak billowing in the wind like some Syd Barret character. Needless to say, the garage-rock band never happened.

What did happen though were nights out at pop up clubs like Blam Blam & State of Grace, gigs at the Railway Club, Julian Cope on mushrooms at the Findhorn Foundation, and lots of free records and tapes. Poor old Julian in his wizard hat. When I tried to interview him, all he could say was, 'the blues are heavy on the vibes man!' Other highlights included Alan Horne of the newly revamped Postcard Records & Mark E Smith of the Fall writing back, and a hilariously long and rambling interview with Eddie Tudorpole (why?). Lowlights included Tom Verlaine's really dull retrospective, 'The Millers Tale', and letting the lads from the Job Enterprise Training Scheme write equally dull reviews of Tekno records. One of the things I got totally wrong across the three issues of *Hype!* was holding up Greenock Faces wannabees Whiteout as the next big thing in after their telly appearance on 'The Word'. They weren't, sadly, although their single 'No Time' is another lost Scottish pop classic.

Hype! Issue 1 1994.

Other misfires which we promoted were various Camden no-hopers like Topper and Pullover and fourth wave punks like The Glory Strummers whom we put on one of our free cassettes. I also never called back the guy from Cornershop, as I reckoned they were indie-duds. So, I was proving to be a very poor scenester indeed. The only band that I championed, who turned out be worth the effort were groovy Giffnock combo, bis, who we've met already. A bouncy group of youngsters who 'combined all the best bits old wave and new wave', as we described them. We stuck a track on one of our cassettes and sent it to John Peel at Radio 1, and surprisingly, we got bis their first radio play for them, and they gave us a shout on their next single. Putting a cover tape on each issue was a good idea, and probably the most fun aspect of producing the zine. It was in essence a throwback to my '80s 'play/record' days. Aside from bis, we had Kilmarnock's criminally underrated Trash Can Sinatras, and Oldham's very own Inspiral Carpets on our free tapes as well. Manda Rin remembers enjoying letting us use her band's tracks. 'The cassette was the level above where you got to actually listen to the bands and create your own opinion. We had great pleasure in letting you use our songs before big labels then owned us and you'd have to seek legal permission'

Bis Cartoon from X124 1996.

There were some good young Scottish bands around during this period, and in many ways it was a high water mark for the autonomous production of self released zines, cassettes, singles and musical happenings. Graham Kemp of Urusei Yatsura very much felt that this was the case. 'It just felt like anyone willing to put in the effort could actually participate. It seems wild now that we could put out 500 records by our friend's bands and sell them all. We found a pressing plant in the Czech Republic and got nationwide distribution despite being very unprofessional and complete naifs in business. It was a world that is just no longer viable. An analogue world fuelled by stamps, cassette tape and cheap copy technology. It helped that we were in Glasgow and everyone we knew were starting bands. The fact that they were often very good bands did no harm. Being well away from the industry, which was/is very centered in the south of England enabled us to have the field all to ourselves. It was there for the taking because the major label vanity indies did not give a fuck for Scottish bands. That only accelerated with Britpop, the whole Tommy Steele, half a sixpence explosion'.

'We did cassettes of Urusei lofi recordings for the shows we put on. There was a period where I had a double tape boombox and ran off live recordings made of the bands at our *Kitten Frenzy* zine nights for free if you sent a C90 and a stamped envelope. I had that in the fanzine and did quite a few. I stopped when it was pointed out that it might not be cool to be sending other people's music, without permission, to which we did not own the rights. In my mind it was purely promotional for the local bands I liked, and I wasn't charging for it, but I think that's fair enough..............'

Kitten Frenzy Zine Presents Courtesy Graham Kemp.

As well as Bis and Uresei Yatsura, another band which we promoted were Spare Snare from Dundee, led by the inimitable Jan Burnett. Resolutely DIY, Jan sent across copies of their first couple of 7" singles released on their own Chute Records. 'Thorns/Skateboard Punk Rocker' came in hand painted numbered sleeve and was pressed as an edition of 617 in three different coloured sleeves, which I particularly liked. I'm pleased to see that in 2005 they were voted the 46th best Scottish band of all time!

By the third issue of *Hype!* we were growing up (a bit) and growing away from just covering music. Our relationship with Highland Printmakers had start to lead us down a bit of a different route, and we thought it would be interesting to produce a zine which covered art and writing as well, but with a point of difference. That difference turned out to be silver heating insulation covers and Tunnocks Caramel Wafers. A call to the local Arts organization where I blagged a few quid, and X124 was more than an idea. As all this was going on, we were hatching other plans too....

The Situationist-lite influence was part of our DNA, having consumed Malcolm McLaren's misinterpretations of Guy Debord's lot for years through punk books and tv docs – Greil Marcus stand up here! We fancied ourselves as northern Dadaists, hence the daft or fake names like Guy Trocchi, Alastair X, Richard Lloyd and Sham 96. It was sometime between 1994 and 1996 that we decided, for a laugh to restyle ourselves as very lightweight art terrorists, the Rust Brothers (name nicked from the remix duo Dust Brothers). Posing as artists, our motto was 'In Rust We Trust', and our first wheeze was the 'Dead Scotsman' postcard which we sent out to loads of Scottish 'celebs' like Wattie from The Exploited, and weirdly, Shirley Manson of Garbage. Why on earth did she reply to us? On the back was one simple question, 'what is Scottish Culture?'. Wattie wrote the witty answer 'shit', while Donnie Munro from Runrig wrote the more opaque, 'hidden under the kilt'. Somehow the ever laconic Adam let us exhibit the results as part of the 250th anniversary of the Battle of Culloden exhibition. The next part of the wheeze was to write to the newspapers moaning about the 'poor taste of the curators', and the childish nom de plumes employed by the bold Rusties. Andy even signed an angry fake letter off as 'James Pursey, Culloden'! The good townsfolk had obviously never heard of, or didn't care about Sham 69. Bizarrely, after this episode, Adam let me loose on the gallery walls where I nailed a stencilled boiler suit to, as part of an installation involving a washing machine and a length of hosepipe.

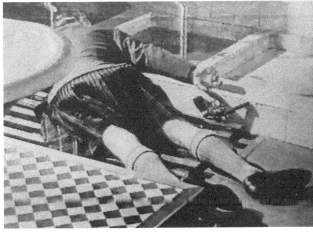

Dead Scotsman –
Image by Andy
Goddard, 1995

On the subject of Situationism, the ever thoughtful Andrew Burnett recalls that 'funnily enough in my youthful exuberance and perhaps naivety I was thrilled to interview The Redskins but unfortunately found the singer to be a bit nasty – considering we were young kids simply trying to do a fanzine interview. Only latterly did I more fully discover the grotesque egoism that permeates and undermines the far left. *Ferocious Apache* and *Close Lobsters* were and are more Situationist than Leftist.'

On with X124. I wrote off to some of my favourite writers like Edwin Morgan and Iain Crichton Smith. Edwin Morgan contributed an excellent interview and Iain CS sent us a poem for publication. We also bagged interviews with writers Duncan MacLean and editor of *Rebel Inc.* Magazine Kevin Williamson, both who had published early work by Irvine Welsh, Alan Warner and Janice Galloway. They had been influenced by the punk ethos, with Maclean's *Clocktower Press* being particularly in debt to zine culture. '*Clocktower* was certainly directly copied off fanzines : the idea of DIY, fast publication – cultural intervention rather than money-making product'. Talking of punk, I was also delighted that Richard Hell, the man who may or may not have invented the punk look as patented by Malcolm McLaren, had also agreed to talk to me.

Adam had been approached by a recent arrival in the Highlands from down under who had seen our zines and wanted to write for us. An aspiring writer, he was keen to scribe something in the 'underground' press. Adam appeared to have taken against him and advised me not to contact him. Needless to say, I did, and he asked to review some books and records for us. What harm could that do? Michel Faber – a strange cove, and no doubt about it! His review of The Three Wise Men E.P by forgotten Glasgow noise rockers, Trout, certainly struck the wrong chord. 'The kindest thing I can say about Trout is that their main man is a talented cartoonist. Their songs are dire...I'd have to say Trout's musical prowess is what I'd expect from a band who prefer to play pissed'. Tom Worthington of Bosque Records, who released the trout E.P, is magnanimous enough to admit to he had to tear the page out of his copy for posterity.

Hell's first novel had just come out and his publicist had arranged for me to interview him whilst he was in London. A big deal for me to interview the man who wrote 'Blank Generation', and the fact that I ended up interviewing Hell from a pay phone in the public bar in the Aultbea Hotel (a long story for another time), made me doubly nervous. Anyway, it went fine. Hell coughed his way through the interview, and disappointingly had nothing much interesting to say. His publisher had of course sent a copy for review, and it duly found its way to a cottage in Portmahomack in Ross-Shire, chez Michel. All was good until Faber sent me his review back. He had totally shredded the book, to the extent that I couldn't bring myself to send a copy of the zine to Hell's publisher. 'When Hell/Mudd observes that 'you can spend all day jerking off as long as you describe it well' he is making an astute point which he himself tends to miss. Hell is closer to Hemingway than Naomi Campbell, but not as close as he thinks. ...what really sinks it is its adolescent obtuseness'.

Of course, I'd interviewed Kevin Williams from *Rebel Inc* mag, so I was somewhat relieved that he went slightly easier on the Rebel Inc book, The Children of Albion Rovers. However, he singled out Irvine Welsh's story, as 'business as usual. Those looking for wit may have their work cut out for them'. Ah well, didn't affect Welsh's future literary career too much... As for Michel Faber, I like to think we set him on his way with his writing career in this country. I'm sure he does too.

The zine was well received at the time. From 'Inverness, a town not normally noted for its underground literary pretensions', as drily noted by the Scotsman newspaper in a review of *X124*, perhaps our only review in a 'national' newspaper. It highlighted the silver cover and attached Tunnocks Caramel Wafer, as well as the writing between the covers in quite a complimentary manner. Giving away Caramel Wafers was probably my proudest achievement during my short lived zine publishing escapade. How the 'sweet fancied jewel red and gold' came to be on the cover is one which I struggle to remember, such is its strangeness.

A gentleman who was known to us, but shall remain nameless was trading in couthy rhyme, under the name of Douglas Dreech. He had produced a number of deathless classics about Fife bus drivers, junkie moths, and a stonker about 'Oor manna praised in syrup folds'. We duly wrote to Tunnocks asking them to provide some freebies in return for us printing this ode 'To A Chocolate Wafer Biscuit'. I could scarcely believe it when the postie delivered eight boxes a couple of weeks later. Either the top people at Tunnocks had a highly developed sense of irony, or they'd never read Mr Dreech's doggerel. I have to admit however, that the last verse puts the National Bard to shame with its sheer poetic genius –

'So molars, canines fare thee well
As Mars and Aero we outsell
In Scotia's glooping glucose hell
We're cocoa cursed
Tae Hades dripping caramel
        Ach, could be worse.....'

....

But what of the actual printed layout of these artifacts we've been discussing at length? Let's go back to the early '70s and the outer London town of Croydon, and that man Jamie Reid again.

Reid's interest in urbanism and the Situationist International drew him into the political sphere, and in 1970 Reid created the Suburban Press. The magazine of the same name, *Suburban Press* ran for six issues from 1970 to 1975, and reached a circulation of 5000 at its peak, before Reid sold up and moved to Lewis. *Suburban Press* offered a searing critique of the reduction of nature to consumer spectacle by Croydon's brutalist town planners

By this point Reid was creating collages that mixed newspaper cuttings, magazine images, watercolour and ink drawings and lettering, an immediate precursor to the style later associated with Punk; as Reid explains: 'A lot of the work that came to the public eye with the Sex Pistols was a result of what I'd learnt on that press'. In later work for both Suburban Press and the Sex Pistols Reid recycled such slogans for his own purposes and attempted to distil the essence of Situationist theory into single images, explaining that he 'was trying to put over the waffle in a visual form; trying, say, to summarise a whole chapter of a book in one image'.

Such DIY techniques, including the detournement of newspaper headlines and photographs and illustrations from advertising campaigns in montages were in part formulated by Reid out of necessity who was unable to afford Letraset at the time. This was echoed from the outset of the punk fanzine revolution in its design aesthetic, not so much deliberately so, but also partially out of necessity. Brian Hogg again 'When I began work on each issue of *Bam Balam* I would lay out all the pictures first, draw lines around them and then type the text in the remaining space. That accounts for all the aberrations whereby bits of sentences e.g.

th-

is

what

happ-

ened

next

appeared down the sides of some of the illustrations. I definitely had a vision of how the pages should look before you actually read it and it was important to me to get as close to that as technical limitations would allow. Each article began with a brief history, followed by a descriptive, impressionist passage on their music (Jon Savage's 'haiku'). A discography completed the feature. Any writing 'style' was influenced by the poet/novelist Richard Brautigan whom I greatly admired. His economic, sparse use of words had a profound effect on me. I also ended many of the pieces at a point before the subject's music, in my opinion, deteriorated. Thus, the Pretty Things' ended with 'S.F. Sorrow'; the Byrds with 'Notorious Byrd Brothers' etc.'

'I really liked the do-it-yourself ethos of the Punk 'zines - somehow the scattered, speedy prose and production was right for the times - and I welcomed their arrival, especially those which concentrated on their own local scenes. However, as time moved on the *Sniffin' Glue* handwritten/ransom note approach turned into a something of a visual cliché. I do wish more had experimented with the layout - it was an artform you could be playful with'.

Regarding the indie zines produced in the 80s, journalist and ex-zine editor, Pete Paphides in Gavin Hogg & Hamish Ironside's excellent book, 'We Peaked at Paper' poses the question 'how was it that you had editors in Edinburgh, the Malverns and Hastings alighting at the same aesthetic?'. Hamish, himself a zine editor of 1990s vintage agrees 'only to a limited extent, because I don't think they were all the same aesthetic. It depended a lot on the editor. Some had more flair for design than others, just as some were better writers than others. And to the extent that there was a common 'look' to zines of a certain period, there would probably be some editors who would want to 'fit in' with that look, and others who would want to do something as different as possible, to make their zines stand out'

Drawing out Brian Hogg's point on the availability, or not of technology, Hamish expands on the theme. 'So if you only have a manual typewriter and are printing it on a photocopier, that tends to determine a lot of the design side of it. Then there are decisions like whether to use Letraset or to hand-letter headings, and how densely you pack the text in, how many images you stick in, etc. To take two contrasting cases: in *Sniffin' Glue*, it looks like Mark Perry has deliberately gone with a kind of anti-design aesthetic, in-keeping with the punk ethos, but in fact, as he told me in the interview in our book, he was trying his best to make it look like a professional magazine! On the other hand, if you look at *Juniper Beri-Beri* or *Pastelism*, it's not trying to look like a professional magazine, but you can just tell that there is a naturally brilliant designer at work'.

Some editors just welcomed the opportunity of freedom afforded to them in producing a zine, like Saskia Holling 'enjoyed the whole creative side of putting together the fanzine, the writing, the artwork, the cutting and pasting, even the photocopying! I wrote a book a couple of years ago called 'Girlsville: The Story of The Delmonas and Thee Headcoatees' and that reminded me of putting together a fanzine. I did all the typesetting and layout as well as the writing. I enjoyed all of that too, and hope to write more music related books'.

Regarding the *Ten Commandments*, Bobby Bluebell had undertaken a design course at the College of Building and Printing in Glasgow, so his approach emphasised that element in construction the zine, rather than the musical content necessarily. 'Design was the most important factor for me, and getting into gigs for free another.. in the end it led to many doors opening, through the fact that it led to me meeting so many people'.

In putting together his zine, Sushil Dade says that when they were writing articles, or designing look of the *Pure Popcorn* fanzine they 'always had our readers in mind. These were our views but without the reader there would be no purpose and we believed this was a shared experience with us. It was always fun to think of new concepts so including cartoons for example alongside interviews/playlists etc was fun, but I always wanted a strong visual sense to the fanzine. Making a concertina style fanzine several metres long required much patience in folding paper and negotiating rolls of sticky tape, but it was well worth the effort. Similarly, presenting a fanzine in the style of a 7" single was such a thrill!'

The first issue of *Jingles The Creep* was also done in a concertina style, and run off one Saturday morning at the Skye & Lochalsh Council offices. 'The concertina idea was a neat, if a bit impractical, solution to make the most of the fact we could only print one-sided', says creator Andy Goddard. Like Suhil's zine there was a lot of Sellotape involved in piecing it all together as neatly as possible. 'I wrote single words on the back of each page that formed a whole phrase when you laid the concertina out flat. I was quite prescriptive about the look, and I never liked the spatterfest look of most zines, with near illegible text. The headline text for Issue 3 was traced off the back of the Janitors 'Thunderhead' E.P, with single letters traced individually to create the desired headline, like 'OPEN ALL HOURS' for the Shop Assistants interview'.

Jingles The Creep courtesy Andy Goddard.

The lads were no less obsessive about the typeface used inside the zine, making sure that the text was centred manually with the typewriter, and in columns as well. The interview questions were in bold, 'which meant racking the typewrite back and retyping the questions a second time to make it look bold...no 'select all' laptop wizardry!'

For ourselves there was a deliberate aesthetic on design. *Hype!* had enjoyed some nice cover design courtesy of the Blam Blam club crew in Inverness, but was let down somewhat by the content, partially due to my laziness. For *X124* the foil cover was a nod to the SI, and Andy's cartoons replaced grainy photos, pinched from the pages of music mags. These factors, along with a more professional approach to cut'n' paste techniques, added up to a better looking zine in my opinion. We conducted an interview with four Scottish bands on record label design, one of whom were Urusei Yatsura, and even had an article on a design team from Glasgow. Design for design's sake! However, with the Dreech poem and a 'fake' poem by one Alan Milarky, which nicked Simple Minds lyrics, our tongues remained, at least partially, in our cheeks.

Hype! and X124 Collage.

Regarding *Kitten Frenzy* zine, Urusei's Graham Kemp tried to balance what was available to use with more mundane economic concerns. 'The fanzine was all very cut'n'paste, but informed (like the music we made) by the equipment available. I was using polaroids and a cheap typewriter for record covers, and panels from comics, coloured paper and 2-colour printing for the fanzines. We wanted it to look as good as we could make it with what we had access to. This was very much an outcome of having very little money. We absolutely had to get our paper costs back. I paid a printer for the first one I did, and was probably still trying to recoup until I did the second one'.

'The zine started in 1989 in the queue for Sonic Youth signing the Daydream Nation album in RAT Records. Everyone I ever subsequently met in Glasgow was somewhere in that queue. I had just moved there a couple of months before for exactly that sort of thing. The band were all mirror shaded New York cool so I broke the ice by asking Steve Shelley to sign for my girlfriend, who thought he was the cutest in the band. They all cracked up, and we had a short chat which I included in Issue Zero of *Kitten Frenzy*, along with a review of their two nights at Strathclyde University. Doing stupid shit like that was the whole impetus for getting *Kitten Frenzy* going. I got an issue out in 1990, then started putting it out more regularly 2 years later once I roped in a few friends and found a Gestetner machine we could use for nothing at Drumchapel Youth Centre'.

'We also started Urusei Yatsura around the same time and we would put on nights at Nice N Sleazy and the 13th Note under the fanzine name. We would put on bands like Lung Leg, Yummy Fur, The Blisters, Hello Skinny in 4-band bills, which we, as Urusei Yatsura would open. We would give away copies of the fanzine to everyone who attended, and use the entry fee to pay our paper costs. The bands would get the rest split evenly among them. One typical night we had Spare Snare, The Delgados, BIS and Urusei all playing. I still have the video of that one. We put out 4 or 5 issues in total between 1992-95 and eventually ended up putting out singles by Pink Kross, Eska and a split Urusei Yatsura/Blisters single on the Modern Independent label'.

When Douglas MacIntyre set up Creeping Bent Records,he seemed to have a vision of a multi-disciplinary approach – music, visuals, writing – and kicked the whole thing off with 'A Leap Into The Void', a multi-media event named after Yves Klein's 1960 photo-montage. 'The Creeping Bent Organisation was definitely influenced by the work of Bob Last and Hilary Morrison at Fast Product/pop:aural, these labels were as much about propaganda and packaging as they were about music. I adopted a similar approach of provocation when Creeping Bent was initiated, we were interested in written and visual output and continued that approach from 1994 till the present'.

'The Erotic Urges of Creeping Bent (BENT 014) was a fanzine put together by Ann Donald and Katy Lironi. It featured written word and photo-montage, it was very primitive and Xerox assembled. Katy and Ann were both interviewed by fanzines and the NME, Katy in the Fizzbombs and Ann with the Shop Assistants), so although they never produced fanzines during the C86 period they were very much part of that culture', says Douglas.

All this stuff would no doubt have our resident punk theorists retro-fitting some Lettrist/Duchamp/George Grosz thinking onto the practicalities of designing and producing zines. Admittedly, editors wanted to produce something which looked good, and brought in art school or second hand design templates, but as Matt Walkerdine of Good Press points out, 'everything is theorised and some people like to think that it is important that we have to get to the bottom of it and put things on a higher pedestal. I guess I'm a designer interested and invested in knowing about production and distribution, so I'm happy to hear about a theorised approach but also very happy to hear more about a practical one. I'm about to do a series of publications, and really the impetus was seeing the low price of the production of a commercial output I was doing and thinking - I'm going to use that format, because it economically sound. .... jump it up as much as you like, research more if you want to, but the content is key, and that, and some DIY flourishes are what really grab me'.

In Hamish Ironside's view, 'some zines look too professional to me. They need to be bit rougher around the edges'. Quite. And I think, printed out too, in my opinion. 'Similar to paper books I think there will always be lovers for a paper zine', agrees Manda Rin 'I suppose the biggest problem with that though, is the cost and marketing involved, as lots more can be done online cheaper and faster, saving paper too. However, record collectors value physical items and I think a good zine is a nice item to treasure too'. Mark Ritchie too is of the view that a zine should look on the rough'n'ready side, 'My zines have always been photocopied rather than printed, and the tapes I put out weren't professionally produced either. I think that used to be a source of shame for me, but now I think it's great. The whole point of doing this stuff is that it's DIY, accessible to all, PUNK ROCK, samizdat. I've written a few indignant letters to people who have slagged me off for doing 'unprofessional' stuff, and *Hiroshima Yeah!* occasionally gets snooty comments because it's 'just' a load of double-sided A4 pages stapled at the top left-hand corner.'

Marc Masters thinks that it may be dependent on what you grew up with, 'my instinct is that a zine is only a zine if it's physically printed on paper. Blogs and webzines and tumblr accounts etc are great too, and often share a lot in common with a print zine, but for me there's a magic to a printed zine you get in the mail or at a record store that is distinct from reading about something online. It feels more special, and more personal - the people making them had to put more time and effort in, and accordingly, the readers had to take the step of seeking them out and paying for them. It gives it a feel of a club of sorts, whereas the web often feels rather impersonal and generic, even when the writing is good - if anyone can see it for free anytime they want, something is lost, though for sure other things are gained as well'.

Katy Lironi agrees with the consensus feeling that a zine should be a physical product, 'ours was definitely old school and photocopied. Cut up and pritt sticked together. I like that aesthetic, I think it's more interesting and creative and hands on. But then again.... We didn't have laptops way back when!'

I'd mentioned in a previous chapter that fanzine editors rarely took any notice of potential copyright issues, and routinely used previously published material such as photographs, headlines and reviews, cut and pasted collage style into their own zines. There was an instance a few years back, where an academic writer, in a book about fanzines, was criticised for failing to either attribute ownership correctly, or attributing any ownership of zines at all. The author also failed to notify the creators of the zines used in the book, which caused controversy due to the fact most authors had no clue their zine was being used. There was an interesting debate online, and in one sense, ironic given how guilty many zine editors, including myself, were of appropriating other people's material.

'Just about everything I used was clipped from music papers', recalls Brian Hogg. 'It was never such a problem back then, especially for *Bam Balam* as the 1960s were seen as prehistoric as far as images were concerned. I sent a copy of the all-Kinks issue to the band & got a reply from their PR saying how much fun they had laughing at the pictures - not a word about copyright!'

Whilst there are doubtless ethical questions which arise, Matt Walkerdine, a zine editor himself, feels that there is a certain degree of hypocrisy at play here. 'Exactly that first sentiment, it was all already done - pinched, taken, shared, spread - but I do think there is weirdly fine line. The academic thing definitely seems to rub people up the wrong way as it appears you're benefitting greatly from something as an academic, but I disagree. Have you seen how many bootleg t-shirt things are around? So, we can make a new t-shirt about Spacemen 3, using their original graphics, sell it for £25+ and its fine? But an 'academic' does similar and it gets everyone's backs up? It seems weird'.

And weird has always been the world in which fanzines inhabit. *Pop Avalanche* zine, back in '87, had even questioned the validity of fanzines themselves, perhaps somewhat provocatively 'You don't need to read it... .we didn't need to write it....we don't need to listen to our records....but we do....do you understand what we're saying? Fanzines are not essential - fatuous views on trivial topics leaning dangerously close to egomania - but the trick is to make them seem to matter....enough to lure you the consumer into buying one at any rate'....Hamish isn't sure whether he agrees 'I like the fact that zines can be irreverent, flippant, whimsical ... but I think you still have to believe your own writing is as important as anyone else's, including all the voices in the mass media. I've always believed that about the zines I've read'. His co-editor Gavin takes a different tack. 'Referring back to Pete Paphides' interview he says a zine should "almost be something that no-one has asked for". It's one of the great things about zines in this age of consumer-focused activity. They've not been market-tested, the editor has no thought of audience demographic beyond people who like the same things as they do. No zines are essential but that's fine and it's part of what appeals about them. They're not worthy, they're pop, throwaway, and should be cheap'.

....

Zines had moved on from just being about punk or indie, and other musical genres such as metal and hardcore were also being covered during this period. One of the longest running rock-based zines was *The Incredible Shrinking Fanzine* run from by Andy McVannan and his pal Dave from 1988 until 2004. 'I remember that we bought a fanzine called *Skull and Crossbones* at a gig in the Venue in Edinburgh. Can't remember who was playing although it may have been a band called Political Asylum. I'm not sure what happened really but me and Dave just kinda got inspired by the fact people were doing stuff like that. So, we decided to do one in our own style I guess. And we had tons of fun along the way'.

The pair felt that these kinds of bands weren't being properly covered by the mainstream press, 'And I guess we got a buzz from covering some really good stuff that was around at the time in Edinburgh and Scotland. But in some ways it was the reverse. We were really electrified at discovering a scene for all that music and we just loved the whole process of creating something of our own. The zine I think became more diverse as each issue went by. In the grand scheme we started to cover a lot of stuff that didn't necessarily fall into a particular bracket or scene. Bands like the God Machine for example. They ended up being a huge favourite of ours'.

The Incredible Shrinking Fanzine went on to sell in fairly large numbers, with Issue 4 having a print run of 1,000. 'Yeah, it's pretty crazy when you think of that now' laughs Andy. 'We just put shit loads of effort in. Going round record shops, comic and book shops asking if they wanted to stock some. A huge part was also Ramsey from AK Distribution who distributed about half of them (500) around the UK and USA'.

Incredible Shrinking Fabzine –
Courtesy Andy MacVannan.

Alongside the many female edited zines which we looked at in the last chapter, the big '90s fanzine in Scotland was the aptly titled *Big Noise*, edited by Martin Kielty, and born out frustration with the lack of traction his band was getting in his hometown. 'In Cumbernauld we had something like 12 bands in a very varied scene from the newfangled indie-pop to the actually nearly new-fangled thrash metal. There were no facilities to provide for that healthy scene. Rehearsal rooms were the community centres, converted schools with huge glass facades that just reflected the noise of the band. There were a couple of music pubs but it wasn't possible to rehearse in them. The only place that nurtured us was Cumbernauld Theatre, and at the time it was constantly under threat of being closed to save money. The people who built and ran the "new town" appeared to have the attitude that you played sports until you were 18 then you went to the pub, and you were grateful for that spectrum of lifestyle'.

He was so ticked off with the suits in the town that he even stood as a local councillor, 'I wound up active in local politics (beat the Tory at a local election!) standing as an independent candidate, just saying, "They have no imagination so they don't want us to have any either."' There was a real desire to communicate a story or message that *Big Noise* had in its aesthetic, which is often coupled with frustration at being in a dead-end small town or being isolated from anything which was happening, and therein lies the real beauty of fanzines in being able to do so.

'In my time I've encountered people I found difficult to work with - because of them, me or both of us - but on the occasions where I knew or discovered they'd started out in fanzines, it always changed everything for me. It meant that even if we disagreed on details, their commitment to telling stories wasn't in question, and that's important to me. It's a get-out-of-jail-free card in my book. I mean why would anyone do that to themselves if they didn't think it was important and valuable work?!' And Martin has a missionary zeal about the atmospherics which a good zine can create. 'Thing is – and I wonder if others agree – I never regarded working in print as a craft; for me it was my art. The images you can put in people heads with words, along with laying those words on a page to present a sense of essential movement... I loved it and still do. For me BN was both the medium and the message, while I think it was less so for others'.

Big Noise started in 1991 and ran through several incarnations, before petering out at the end of the decade. 'At that point it was a case of nicking photocopies from the community centre where I worked part-time. I'm sure they knew it was happening but in the spirit of promoting community enterprises, a kindly blind eye was turned'. By the second and third iterations of the zine, Martin was employed at the Scottish tabloid, The Daily Record, and tried the same trick again. 'I was daring to use the colour copier at the Record, to make posh colour covers, and the toner from the cheaper mono copied we'd used for the interior melted inside the colour machine, causing expensive damage and leading me to be advised by a friendly older journalist that I was making a "career-limiting move" if I continued...'

But, there were overriding aesthetic and cultural concerns which trumped such trivia. 'I never really took America seriously as a cultural movement, and I still don't, but if you came from America to here, or went from here to America, that was *Big Noise* territory. I rather think of that as a large-minded idea, although some people might think it's small minded. It felt like a respectful exchange of art and ideas between equals, although perhaps not financially... which, of course, has no place in art anyway'.

Chapter 8 :

Millenium Psychosis Blues (or making the old new)

Two fallacies persist around DIY Culture. Firstly, that cassettes and cassette culture is dead, and secondly, that zines are a thing of the past. Neither of these statements is true, as we'll discuss in this chapter.

Before talking about these though, it's important to acknowledge the crate-digging efforts of Michael Train in the early 2000's. His 'Kilt by Death : Sound of Old Scotland' CDr was mentioned briefly in conjuction with the 'Sad Day We Left The Croft' album, but it's absolutely necessary to expand on this. Listening to it in one sitting it 'makes a pretty convincing case for Scotland's inclusion alongside New Zealand as one of the most consistently committed DIY outposts'. That quote comes from author David Keenan's sales listing from his, now defunct, Volcanic Tongues shop and record label. Michael explains in more detail. 'He's written a foreword for my Discography book, which should be out soon. The book is 'Gimme Your Heart: A Scotland Punk and New Wave Discography (1977–1984)'. The foreword is 'Total Liberation from the Tyranny of Received Anything'. I think it's valid, though the DIY spirit was strong in many places at the time. Scotland is in some sense the first frontier, and it's too perfect that there is a border. I was sensitive to that having grown up in Maine, which is sometimes thought of that way in its relation to Massachusetts, from which it split. And there's a bit of Celtic treble rebellion afoot... As well as just the standard centre-and-periphery relation to London that isn't uncommon in the regional post-punk response to London's call. True also for New Zealand—where it's felicitous that Dunedin and Edinburgh are cognate'.

'Kilt By Death : The Sound of Old Scotland

The story on how KBD came into being is an interesting one, and is a masterclass in rooting out lost and forgotten DIY recordings. 'I was a DJ in the Rock Department (known as 'Record Hospital' or 'RH') at WHRB, the station affiliated with Harvard University in Cambridge, Massachusetts. It's a department devoted to punk obscurity, and the overall station has a tradition of deep dives into specific artists, labels, and scenes twice a year during what is called a 'Reading Period' These take place after classes have ended for the semester but before exams and are called 'Orgies'. That Rough Trade Orgy had been so successful in uniting the various factions of RH that we were looking for another with similar sweep—punk, pop, art, noise. I remember the Scrotum Poles' 'Radio Tay' popping up on a comp and a record store clerk's handing me the first Valves 7". So, Scotland was in the air. Also, my ancestry is a combination (on my father's side) of Irvine and Inverness, so maybe Scotland was more on my brain than, say, Spain'. And finding out about, and assembling the compilation became a massive undertaking, a labour of love for rare vinyl and cassettes. 'To learn about the bands, we read the Department's copy of Volume—The International Discography of the New Wave cover to cover and noted possibilities. We were also hugely assisted by having access to Chuck Warner's collection and sales catalogs, which he could search electronically. He was living nearby and had the deepest stock of British DIY in the US. He would later start Hyped to Death and do the Messthetics collections, the Scotland one included. He loaned us hundreds of rare records for the broadcast. I remember his giving us at least two copies of the Scrotum Poles' EP so that we could segue tightly from song to song without dead air'!

'Eventually this became a 95-hour retrospective of the Scottish underground from 1977 to 1994, with the first hours devoted to early DIY. These were bands like Fire Exit, Fun 4, Freeze, One Takes, Metropak, Strutz, Those Intrinsic Intellectuals, and the One Takes. Another section focused on Fast and Pop Aural bands—Fire Engines, Scars, Restricted Code, Flowers…. And then on to better-known groups like the Rezillos, Exploited, Shop Assistants…'…….

'Later in the 90s, as I saw Chuck putting out cassettes compiling amazing 7"s, I started making my own Scotland cassette mixes for friends. And I got some technical advice from him… Over time, that evolved to CDrs as the tech got more accessible, and then the lightbulb went off. Initially, I had in mind three thematic CDs: punk, art, pop. But I've always been annoyed by the Balkanization in collecting, so eventually I went chronological—to make the collector scum listen to the Venigmas'.

It's very much a collection of the hand-glued, xeroxed and self released, as Michael himself outs it, but it without a doubt helped to re-ignite some interest in the more dusty and forgotten corners of Scottish punk, post-punk & indie. And it was never his intent to make any money from the project. 'I gave the comp at no charge to anybody who came calling. I think we sold or gave away more than 300 and fewer than 500 Maybe 50 went as donations to WFMU for fundraising?'. And future compilers certainly owed a debt of gratitude for his diligence. 'It's interesting now, with so much more knowledge at hand, to read back to the state of things in 2004/5, but I think it holds up overall; the first couple of Big Gold Dream CDs from the Cherry Red box certainly have a lot of overlap'!

....

Taking a look at contemporary DIY cassette scene, it's important to recognise that the largest portion of contemporary self-released and second-hand cassettes are distributed through the two online platforms Bandcamp and Discogs, & the majority of currently released cassettes are professionally produced. This is a change from the '80s and '90s where homegrown cassettes graced the covers of fanzines. The significance of the cassette has changed and in the 21st century, it is first and foremost offering a re-establishing of physical relationships with music.

An investigation of cassettes in Glasgow's and Edinburgh's Independent Music landscape in which the usage of cassette tapes by younger generations is critically assessed by older scene members, offer the notion that cassettes are a serious option for the release of DIY music. Moreover, Taylor's Academic Paper, 'From Analogue to Digital', written in 2014 which traces development of the cassette in the Scottish independent music scene, comes to the following conclusion. 'The cassette is a 'hybrid thing' which has been subjected to a transformation of 'pragmatism to symbolism' in which cassette tapes are not primarily consumed as practical audio formats for music listening but as symbolic tokens that represent devotion: participants did not actually listen to the cassettes that they were buying, but rather, listened to the digital download that accompanies the vast majority of postmillennial cassette releases'. (Taylor, 2014, p. 2).

Johnny Lynch puts it, perhaps more succinctly, from a musician's standpoint. 'Tapes are fun, because they are relatively cheap to make, they are largely manufactured within the UK (so the carbon footprint is less), and you can have them made in a variety of interesting colours. These days, the physical artefact is something that sits on a shelf, and possibly never gets played - the customer will likely use the download code that comes with each copy, or even more likely just stream the music from their platform of choice'.

106

Lost Map Records Collage.

Taylor's academic study backs up Johnny's experience. 'Participants emphasised the cassette as a convenient and cheap way of catering for their desire for a physical thing. The majority of them highlighted that even though they were aware that they could access the same music online for free, the purchasing and ownership of a certain cassette is important as a means of putting money in the hands of the artists and labels that you enjoy. It becomes a symbolic token of your involvement with a scene, as a person who doesn't merely observe or listen, but instead is an active participant in independent music who actively contributes to the production of culture'. (Taylor, 2014, p. 2). Or again, as Johnny puts it, 'People want to buy the physical thing because they know it directly supports the musician. The more limited edition you can make the physical artefact, the more it's worth to the fanbase'.

Multi-media artist Ruaridh Law takes a slightly different view in the resurgence of cassettes and their role in being an 'artifact' or 'product'. 'It's definitely not true for me; I buy cassettes fairly often and listen to every one of them. I'm not wild at all on that precociousness about "art" artifacts - tapes are there to be played, prints are there to be displayed, booklets are there to be read. I've never created or released something as a placeholder - they always have a practical use and I would hope that that's how people are interacting with them'.

He does however, acknowledge the difficulties in shouting above the (tape) noise, but thinks that there is a way through the maze. 'I can't speak for everyone, but at its most simple: as it's becoming harder and harder to attract attention from others to do things for you (like release your record,

107

publish your book, exhibit your photography), its simpler to set your sights on a smaller audience and do it yourself, free from compromises. I think as technology or software or whatever has improved to a level where anyone can make a film, or write something, or put music together, so too the people creating this stuff aren't feeling hamstrung by medium or genre. You can easily get a group of likeminded people via social media or in person who are all into each other's stuff, and creating for the benefit of 100 people you know will like it and that will support you to in turn support them becomes the new "success" i think'.

'Financial success is all but impossible anyway apart from the 1% at the top and therefore creative freedom, without restrictions, and with a 1-1 relationship with the people enjoying what you do I think is the proper fulfilling way to measure success'.

The re-release of Edinburgh trio Young Father's debut 'mixtape' TAPE ONE and it's follow up TAPE TWO in 2017, allowed a reappraisal of two albums that sat firmly outside the mainstream in 2011/12 and still seem prescient today. TAPE ONE was recorded within a week. It was first released in November 2011 as a free download and limited edition cassette with individually spray-painted sleeves. TAPE TWO was recorded almost immediately afterwards, in January 2012. Eventually LA based label Anticon picked up both albums and gave them a limited release in the USA, reinforcing Ruaridh's view about validating and personalising the consumption of tapes for customers.

And that aspect of several artistic disciplines rolled up into one product was a motivator in the setting up of the Akashic tape label set up by Ollie and Laurie Pitt in 2011 as a DIY vehicle for releasing their own music. 'I was interested in having an outlet for totally over the top, hand-made packaging', says Ollie. 'The first release was housed in a triangular, screen printed hand sewn sleeve with lino cut inserts. It's the kind of thing that takes so long to make, it would never be commercially viable - but if you're doing it for yourself, for your own music, on your own label that will probably never turn a profit then it feels worthwhile'.

Akashic Records Cassette Release courtesy Akashic Records.

Keith McIvor aka JD Twitch is a producer, DJ and record label owner amongst other things. He runs the Optimo label in Glasgow and its multiple offshoots. In 2021 he began releasing the Optimo Music Tape series, 'These Tapes Are Made For Walking', ten mix cassettes which also contained a suggestion for a walk in or around Glasgow. Keith has long been an advocate of access to music for everyone, and that legacy inspired him to get involved with the production of this series. 'I always cite the example of how I read about and became fascinated by Fela Kuti circa 1981. I was always looking out for his records but never found any and had no way to hear his music. I finally heard him when some of his albums finally got reissued in 1997. It took me 16 years to hear him.'

'My inspiration to start the series of tapes came about during the pandemic. Two things happened at once. I was having a clear out and found my old Walkman and a bag full of tapes and also started going on daily long walks. I'd walk ten miles every day (something I continue to do) and started listening to all these old tapes of mine. I really enjoyed the format again so decided to make a series of mix tapes designed to accompany a walk and thought I'd put them on Bandcamp and see how they went. They are easy to get made and have a fast turnaround. I was blown away by the response and struggled to keep up with demand'.

The label also put out a fanzine in aid of Foodbanks that sold out it 2 x100 copy run. '*Poets for Sale* was actually the idea of my designer, Andrew Beltran, who suggested it and put it together, and I contributed to it. There may be a follow up one day. I was a keen consumer of fanzines back them, and a lot of them I can't remember. Ones I still have copies of include *Vague, Underground, Re/Search, Neuemusik & Strange Things Are Happening*'. But he believes that this generation have killed off the sacred musical cows of the past, and that this is a very positive thing. 'I was an evangelist for electronic music at a time when a lot of people were resistant to it. I was big into dub too, and a lot of Noise Rock/No Wave. I really admire how knowledgeable and open minded a lot of young people are now. There is also a lot less respect for the musical 'canon' which I think is a good thing...create your own canon'.

There's an engaged radicalism permeating much of the city's music that manifests in its small-run tape labels. Lauren Thomson runs Heavenly Creature, recently described as 'chronicling the universalities of heartache, getting by, friendship, and solidarity'.

Lauren agrees, and says that her aim of the label is for 'people to think of community when they think of Heavenly Creature; of what music can be a vehicle for and how it can create change in a world that is very complicated and hard to navigate'.

109

And on Glasgow's DIY scene she has this to say. 'It's has always been my favourite city in the world, even when it wasn't home to me. There's always been such a sense of DIY and community — whatever that means — and I'd felt it even three hours up the road in the secluded countryside. I'd been pretty enamoured by Postcard Records and the idea that you could just do whatever you wanted from the comfort of your bedroom with your friends. Starting the label catapulted me into a whole new world of creatives, and it's where I've found myself flourishing and making real long lasting connections. Struggletown and GoldMold in particular are two incredible platforms making so much happen in the current Glasgow scene — Gary and Steven from these labels have become close friends of mine and put a real effort into maintaining a real DIY ethos in everything they do.

'Glasgow has such a rich history with DIY labels and zine publishing, current and not-so-current: Postcard, Vesuvius Records, Night School, Glasgow Zine Library. There's a mindset of "I want to make this happen, so I will" in the city that resonates above everything else. I think that has always been the case and it's really important that the space for community still thrives' And Ollie Pitt emphasises the creative aesthetic of the city. 'Glasgow has always been a great place for crossover between the visual arts and music. I have no idea if it's any better now than in the past, but it has always been an unpretentious and open minded place. Compared to a lot of other cities, the arts and music in Glasgow are comparatively free from commercial interests. This helps communities from around scenes and engenders a DIY ethos'.

And as for cassettes themselves Lauren says that 'physical media is all I really spend money on outside of necessities - I think owning what you love in the digital age is really, really important and I'd always loved the idea of getting to curate something physical myself, I just hadn't known how to go about it. Cassettes felt like the most obvious choice - covid meant there was a severe backlog and wait time when working with vinyl pressing plants and a friend of mine was able to dub cassettes himself, so it just made sense'.

And there has been a second life for the Kilt By Death series as well, this time in cassette and printed matter form, and with a hand in the arrival of the 'Big Gold Dream' film in the USA. The film essentially documents the story of Scotland's post-punk scene, focusing on record labels Fast Product and Postcard Records, and was released in 2015. Michael had met writer Sukhdev Sandhu through a friend. 'He had always found it so unlikely that two US college students had taken such a plunge into Scottish obscurity back in 1994 that he had us sit down and interview each other for the booklet, Hysteric Esoterics (from an unreleased Those Intrinsic Intellectuals song), that came with Kilt By Death 4'. The cassette itself came with 27 tracks that hadn't made it onto the original KBD compilation back in 2005. He was in touch with the people working on the movie and arranged to be the first person to present it in the US'.

KIlt By Death 4 - Cover & Inlay Courtesy Michael Train.

....

With the rise of the internet in the mid-1990s, zines had started to fade from public view, partially due to the ability of web pages to fulfil much of the role of personal self-expression, and some print zines transformed themselves into web-zines. At the same time it's fair to say that the mainstream music press was dying a death during the first few years of the 21st Century. *Vox* Magazine had folded in 1998, and a year later *Select* also shut up shop. *Melody Maker*, which had originally launched in 1926, followed *Select* by a couple of months. From a circulation of 300,000 at its height, it went with a whimper, with barely 20,000 copies being sold at the end. The NME soldiered on for a decade before being brought to a final halt in 2018. However, and unexpectedly, since about 2010, there has been a resurgence in alternative printed publications along with the rise of zine fairs and zine libraries across the country.

Glasgow Zine Fair was one of the first in Scotland, and has been running since 2013. Chloe Henderson of Coin Operated Press, who print and produce zines for themselves and others, sees Zine fairs as fantastic resource for makers. 'Yeah, every little niche is covered - if you want to see a zine on a certain topic, there is almost certainly one out there that exists, and the best place to look is in a zine fair! Zine-making is on the rise, and with that, there are more and more zine fairs - which is great to see. Certainly, since the pandemic we have noticed an uptake in folks making and being interested in zines, and we are super happy to see that. I think it stems from a need for connection, and a focus shift to the smaller, more important things in life that folks were maybe neglecting pre-pandemic.' Chloe stresses that Coin Operated Press 'value intersectional feminist culture and we're especially interested in working with the LGBTQ + community, and those with chronic illnesses and disabilities.

Zine culture is all about diversity and we welcome people of all genders, sexualities, ages, races, abilities, and backgrounds to get involved in Coin-Operated Press. I hope people find connection and creativity through our zines and through our workshops... that's our main aim'! She adds that, 'I would LOVE to collaborate with a musician to bring out a cassette to go along with a zine - if any musicians out there want to work on a collaboration, do hit us up!!'

Lauren Thomson's own work has cut across zines as well, and sees them as part of an integrated and larger whole in Scotland's thriving music scene. 'I've made a few zines, the first of which was a project I worked on with a friend overseas who mostly illustrated whilst I worked on the written content. We did a few issues, and our goal was to shine a light on marginalised and lesser known artists within DIY music scenes. I also created a zine with a friend from NYC during lockdown which documented what isolation looked like for queer people across the globe using self portraits and small text excerpts'.

And there are still a number of music focussed print zines around. Mark Ritchie has continued to produce them since his *Splish! Slash! Splosh!* in the indiepop boom of the 1980s. 'In the early 2000's I started a zine called Sniper Glue which then changed its name to *Hiroshima! Yeah.* I've been doing that ever since and we're currently nearing our 200th issue. *Hiroshima! Yeah* is mostly poetry, prose and personal writing disguised as music reviews, though we've also done memorable interviews with Withered Hand, Julie Doiron, Mark Eitzel, Willy Vlautin and Frankie Stubbs.

Good Press is a Glasgow-based bookshop and art space specialising in independently produced publications and projects, the foundation of which is its open submission policy. This means that it can stock the work which is playful, fun, challenging, and reminiscent of a punk mentality that insists on a distinctly DIY attitude. 'We do not operate a curatorial selection. Curating a selection means imposing our views on others, which goes against our mission, says Matt Walkerdine. 'The open policy stems from thoughts around rejecting individual taste and ensuring freedom for all. We accept and put for sale any printed matter we receive, as long as it is not harmful or discriminatory to others', and its 'not-for-profit' policy is the core of Good Press' ethos. Sixty-five percent of each sale goes to the artist or maker, while thirty-five percent goes to fund the space, its rent, bills, and maintenance.

He also runs his own publishing offshoot, *The Grass Is In the Fields For You*, which combines the ethics of Good Press with the DIY zine ethic. The title is taken from a song by The Revolving Paint Dream, and early release on Creation Records, and aims to use 'approachable means of mass-production exploiting their generous flaws and integrating low-technology detailing in inventive ways'. As a graphic designer by trade, he feels that mass production is important to what he does, and also important to Good Press in a sense. 'One of the caveats of the open policy being we won't stock one-offs, or artworks. We're interested in the next step of small press, almost the 30 upwards print count, which is still very small of course, but it's the dual aspect of satisfaction for the maker – when you make many, the achievement is high – when an individual comes into a shop and it's not highly limited or expensive, then that's good for them. Mass production was of course a factor to Creation Records, and Alan McGee would have wanted to get music into as many hands as possible'.

Matt ensures that all *The Grass Is In the Fields For You* publications are open-edition, meaning that they won't go out of print, and that he is free to reprint in a different style or print method. His thinking is that the individual texts may age in style, but that shouldn't affect the content or the audience perception. The press also represents a place for him to experiment with design aspects, both in formal and informal design but additionally with production. 'It's above all for fun and personal experimentation, which revolves around my own taste aesthetically, and if that comes out DIY, again, that's where I come from'.

Entrances Uncovered courtesy Matt Walkerdine.

Looking back to the zine and cassette packages of the '80's and '90's, Lauren Thomson would like to push them to the forefront of her label. 'I've done the odd thing here and there but it took a little bit of a backseat — I started a new job and moved home and time to work on the label was limited. Just recently I'd thought about want I want the label to look like moving forward and I want there to be a heavier focus on physical written content — zines and inserts and the like. We did a co-release with Dead Hound Records for Loup Havenith's first record which included a cassette and zine package and I've been wanting to work on something similar ever since'.

Lost Map records have also submerged themselves in the zine/print/music crossover in an effort to connect with the listener, 'you want them to enter your world' says Johnny Lynch. 'One of my favourite zines was for an album we released by a French artist called Clémentine March, who created a hand-drawn lyric and chord chart zine. It looked so cool. These items are especially handy for releases on CD, as so little value is placed on a stand-alone CD these days'. The zine aesthetic seems to fit so well with the whole Lost Map ethos, that I wondered if perhaps a regular zine was something which they might consider producing? 'We have a label subscription series called Post Map Club. Every month we send members 3 postcards, containing download codes for new music from different artists on the roster, alongside a printed newsletter from me. This scratches that zine itch, for me - the postcards look really cool, the artists can get really inventive with the images, and they feel uniquely collectible too'.

Clementine March CD & Zine courtesy Lost Map Records

Optimo Records 25ᵗʰ anniversary album, released in 2024 rounded up, not just sonically, but presentationally all of the label's influences with the classic post-punk accoutrements of a fanzine, badge & yellow vinyl. Keith McIvor acknowledges the debt to Fast Product and Postcard, but rather than the label stamp its design aesthetics on the artists, he's taken the view of having that vision for the label, but incorporating it with the artists' own creative input. 'I'd say about 50% of the artists I work with had / have a strong sense of design so they've had input into how their records look. Perhaps historically, the majority of people making records were happier for the label to just get on with it?'

Then there is the enduring appeal of punk rock, which really kicked off the fanzine boom, except these days it's gone around the globe several times and back. '*Screaming Punk Planet* was born out of my own research into punk movements across the globe', says zine maker Dave Emmerson. 'It got to a point that I'd found so many musical gems that I felt like I'd be wrong not to share it in some way with others. I started laying out maps of continents, then countries, with info about the bands & labels I'd discovered using a cut and paste punk flyer kind of aesthetic. Lots of pritt sticks go into making that zine. It's moved more into a phase of interviewing punks from across the globe and reviewing albums – all in the hopes of sharing the treasure I've found with others'.

Skreaming Punk Planet Punk pop edition –
Courtesy Dave Emmerson.

Talking about things going full circle, I've decided to round off this alternative of history of Scottish fanzines and DIY music culture with Brian Hogg, the man who kickstarted the whole fanzine revolution north of the Border. Brian published his seminal book 'All That Ever Mattered : The History of Scottish Pop & Rock' in 1993, which is sadly long out of print now, but perhaps due a revamp I wondered? 'All That Ever Mattered' grew out of 'Beatstalking', a six-part BBC Radio Scotland documentary, produced by my close friend Stewart Cruickshank. I did some research for the early episodes and the idea for a book evolved from that. Initially the BBC were considering publication but that fell through and I then hit a seemingly insurmountable problem - UK publishers were reluctant to touch something purely about Scotland, and Scottish publishers were wary of anything 'pop'. Eventually Guinness took up an option following my work on their 'Encyclopaedia of Popular Music' and it duly appeared in 1993.'

'I can't believe it's now 30 years old, and that almost as much time has now passed as the book itself covers. There have been one or two approaches about a revised version but they each fell through because I insisted it should either be reprinted as is, with factual corrections and a short 'what's happened since' epilogue but still closing circa 1990, or I begin again, bringing everything up-to-date where applicable. The notion of tacking on a few chapters covering say, Belle & Sebastian, Franz Ferdinand and Chemikal Underground, and leaving Teenage Fanclub at 'Bandwagonesque' seemed ridiculous but that indeed was suggested, as well as asking KT Tunstall to write an introduction.'

'I now feel it's much too late to house the subject in a single volume with the kind of detail I put into the original. Too much has happened. Vic Galloway wrote 'Rip It Up' for the exhibition of the same name, but it's a primer rather than a forensic history. I'm very proud of 'All That Ever Mattered' - written pre-World Wide Web - but I'm quite happy it stays where it is. If someone wanted to republish along the lines of 'Scottish Rock & Pop 1955-1990' then fine but, if not, so be it. The title was indeed taken from the Shop Assistants' song, although other commentators cited another of the same title by Orange Juice. I find that ambiguity most appealing'.

'Scotland, and Edinburgh in particular, produced some of Post-Punk's finest bands. Fire Engines were incredible, so too Josef K, but the city also gave us Metropak, the Visitors, the Flowers and Scars, whose 'Adult/ery' single is another of the period's best. This continued well into the 80s - Glasgow and its environs had the Pastels, Primal Scream and the whole Bellshill shebang, while back along the M8 there were the Shop Assistants, Jesse Garon & the Desperadoes, the Delmontes, the Vultures and that's just the tip of a thriving iceberg. They were prolific and exciting times. By then, however, 'Bam Balam' had folded. Labels such as Edsel, Bam Caruso and Ace/Big Beat – among many others – were reissuing the kind of records I had been writing about and I felt the magazine was now redundant. I was also writing liner notes to many of their compilations, thus fulfilling a similar function. Of course, nowadays time is folding in on itself and there's greater effort put into recycling the past than promoting the future. I hate to think that I played any small part in that sorry process.....' Despite his, admittedly valid reservations, research for this book has demonstrated that the lively and vibrant culture of zines, small labels and the cassette underground will ensure that new music will continue to evolve, mutate, and have an important place in Scotland for years to come.

And of *Bam Balam*, I suggested to Brian that he could go the same way as Mark Perry and Tony Drayton, compiling their zines into book format. Given the thriving DIY scene currently, perhaps there isn't any need to wallow in nostalgia. He sensibly had this to say. 'We'll see what happens reference a 'bound' *Bam Balam*. Sometimes you lose the wonder & mystery, so to speak, by making things available again. There's a magic to memories.........

Appendix :

A–Z zine listing and info

We've taken a drive down the highways and byways of Scotland, and indeed jumped on a few ferries and passing place roads as well, just to get to this point in the book.

Before punk, Scotland was a cultural backwater musically, pretty much ignored by critics and label bosses and A&R men south of the border. Things began to change slowly with record labels such as Fast Product and Postcard allowing a distinctive style and approach to evolve, proving that you didn't have to necessarily move to London. Other smaller labels and DIY cassettes helped to spread the message more widely. Fanzines allowed a discourse around music which was previously the preserve of music journalists, and the breakdown of barriers belatedly allowed women their own distinctive voice, both in making music and writing about it.

With this in mind, I've put together what I hope is a reasonably exhaustive list of music, and music related zines from the period of 1975-2025. The whole thing was kicked off by *Bam Balam* which started in 1975, quickly followed by the pioneering punk zines. Some zines were probably copied in runs of tens, whilst others sold several thousand copies, but all of them, no matter how small have had an important part to play in the narrative of the nation's musical development.

I must mention several online blogs which have been an invaluable resource in starting to compile this listing. Of particular note are 'For Malcontents Only' and 'Still Unusual'. If you get the chance to look them up, please do, as they are a veritable goldmine of information, not just about zines, but music in general. also need to mention the Glasgow Zine Library and Glasgow Women's Library who provide another useful source of information. And of course, the many individuals who shared their fanzines with me.

It just remains for me to sincerely apologize for any I may have inadvertently missed. If this book is ever reprinted, I promise to rectify my mistake, and include them on a future edition. See below 50 years of Scottish music zines!

100%

A 1990s zine. Issue 1 has an interview with Bikini Kill, and stuff on Belle & Sebastian, poetry, cartoons and reviews. Not sure if further issues were ever produced

23621

A 1980s Greenock based zine from Café Information Central, which was a drop-in centre in the town. Encouraging all aspiring writers, musicians etc to contribute......

A Boring Fanzine:

This well designed zine was produced by the label Boring Records and Bishopbriggs punk band The Exile, who also ran the label. The first issue came out around the time of the release of the band's Don't Tax Me E.P. in August 1977. One of the tacks, Jubilee, made it onto the Messthetics compilation CD, which, as the sleevenotes stated, 'focuses on a brief, intense scene of ardently independent bands who got started rubbing shoulders with 1977 punk, then paid no attention at all to London. London returned the favour'. The zine later changed its name to *Plain Sailing*.

Alive and Kicking:

There were at least two fanzines in the late 1970s with this title, one from Glasgow and one from Stirling. Did Simple Minds steal the title for their live album? Possibly. The Glasgow one appeared to exist around 1978. Johnny Waller wrote a review on post-punk band Wire in it. No further information seems to be out there

Alternatives to Valium

Started by Alastair MacKay from university in Aberdeen in 1983. NME gave ATV a good write up, as did Tony Fletcher's fanzine Jamming! There were five issues and by the final one he was printing 1000 and selling most of them.

Anarchoi

A hardcore punk zine from Kilwinning that was running around 2005 and featured the likes of the Lurkers, the Disruptors, Drongos For Europe, Abusive Youth and Intimidation Records.

Angry

An anarcho-zine produced by Chris Low from Stirling in 1983 which ran for one issue only. It was originally intended to have been included with the Apostles 'Smash the Spectacle' EP.

Anatomia

A 1993 old skool death metal zine, edited by Bill from *Pulveriser*.

An Extra Boring Fanzine

A one-off special of *A Boring Fanzine* for the Christmas of 1977. There is an advert for the Backstabbers notorious 'Exmas Party' at Maryhill Community centre with the pre-Orange Juice, Nu-Sonics, which ended in a near riot. See Simon Goddard's Postcard Records book for a hilarious, if undoubtedly exaggerated account of the shenanigans.

Another Tuneless Racket

A 70s punk zine from East Kilbride retailing for 20p. It featured mainly punk bands, with particular emphasis on local acts like The Stillettoes, The Electrix and the Sinister Turkeys! The Turkeys, as I'll call them, appeared on the Sunset Gun audiozine cassette. There is one currently on sale for online £45. Surely punk was never about that? Gave its name to a book about punk. Also, were turkeys ever sinister?

Anty-Gravity

Issue 1 came out in 2002, produced by Laura from Abington and featured reviews of Easyworld, Feeder, Helen Love, Muse, King Adora, Crackout, The Donnas and Murray the Hump amongst others. Interviews with McKlusky, Ballboy, Purple Munkie, Union Kid and Monkey Steals the Drum.

Arsing About:

A freebie zine that appeared now and again (see *Wrong Image)*.

Asylum

An Edinburgh based 1980s zine run by Fritz Van Helsing. No relation to Lenny Helsing of The Thanes, in fact, Fritz was originally from Inverness and moved to Edinburgh at the start of punk, changing his name by deed poll en-route. (Again, see *Wrong Image*).

Asylum Jingles

Eighties Indie zine from Dumbarton. Syd Barrett fans by the looks of it. Also covered bands from the west of Scotland, such as The Dragsters from Greenock

Away From The Numbers

Brian Hogg's 1977 was already two years into producing *Bam Balam*, which focused on 1960s pop and psychedelia . He didn't want to turn *Bam Balam* into something it wasn't, so the new zine, named after Brian's favourite Jam song, allowed him to simultaneously cover the emerging punk scene and 'the excitement of the new music'. He very quickly tired of The Jam, and Paul Weller's 'one dimensional voice', and also their appropriation of the Union flag.

Baby Honey

Part of the Sha-la-la collective of zines across the UK who distributed flexi discs with their zines with no help from distribution companies. *Baby Honey* Issue 1 gave away a rather excellent flexi featuring Glasgow's Clouds (who later featured Norman Blake of Teenage Fanclub fame)

Bam

An Eighties zine edited by Josef K's manager Allan Campbell.

This was a well produced zine which covered both film and music. Allan Campbell played a key role in the Edinburgh music scene of the time, having also managed the Delmontes and founded his own label, Rational Records. He was also promoting local gigs including The Associates' first ever show and booking groups including Orange Juice, Aztec Camera, The Fall, Teardrop Explodes, New Order and Echo and the Bunnymen at Valentino's in Edinburgh

Bam Balam

This fanzine was one of the formative influences on Mark Perry in setting up his *Sniffin' Glue* zine. Brian Hogg's motivation for creating Bam Balam was actually quite similar to that of the early punk fanzine writers. He was bored with the music scene of the mid-1970s, and inspired by reissue compilations like "Nuggets: Original Artyfacts from the First Psychedelic Era, and US zines like *Who Put The Bomp*. Issue 1 came out in February 1975. He named it after a song by perennial underachievers The Flamin' Groovies.

Brian retired *Bam Balam* in 1982 after 14 issues. There had been a news story that Paul Weller had wanted to do a book based on the Bam Balam articles, but nothing came of it, which was Weller's doing. (see interview with Brian Hogg in Chapter 1 of the book).

Beatstalking

Don't know much about this one, apart from it came out in the 1980s and covered bands like Baby's Got a Gun and Toxik Ephex. Billed itself 'The All Scottish Zine'

Beyond the Gutter

A late 1980s anarcho zine which is most notable for the resurrection of comic anti-hero Ivor The Anarchist (see *Ivor The Anarchist* zine)

Bicycle Pump

This was a Grangemouth based zine which helped promote many local bands in the late 1970s. I found a copy of Issue 3's cover online, which retailed for the startling price of 12 new pence originally. It came with a free tape apparently, but this may be a mythical artifact. Who knows?

Blow Your Nose on This

An Alastair Mackay of *Alternatives to Valium* fame zine from the Eighties.

Bigwig

I'm not sure if this was a posh fanzine, or a magazine masquerading as a fanzine. I remember writing some reviews for it in the mid-90s, so it did exist in reality, not just in the dusty vaults of my mind. They ran the oddly titled 'America's Most Vaunted', which was a series of profiles of the leading indie labels in the USA. The trail runs cold thereafter.........

Big Noise

A big selling fanzine which morphed into a professional magazine for a period in the '90s. Run by the now 'canal booze cruising' Martin Kielty, who may or not be planning writing more books about pop & rock

Bittersweet

An A5 zinc. Started in 1994 by MoMo in Glasgow, also known as Maureen Quinn of the Glasgow band, Lungleg.

Boa

A5 Glasgow zine run by Gayle, with Issue 1 coming out in 1995. Issue 2 featured Sally Skull, Urusei Yatsura and Sarah Records, reviews & short stories.

BOF (Boring Old Fart)

A short lived zine from, Edinburgh. Issue 1 reviewed what had happened music wise during 1977 and featured The Rezillos amongst others.

Bombs Away Batman

A fanzine created in 1983 by Grant Morrison from East Kilbride. He reckoned that that the TV Personalities could have been bigger than the Beatles. Well, yeah....

Born Yesterday

A 1981 Glasgow zine. Features an Alan Horne interview, who when asked of the 'so-called Scottish scene' stated, 'There's no such thing. There just happens to be the best bands in Britain coming from Scotland, mainly Orange Juice, Josef K and the Fire Engines. This doesn't happen because of the media – journalists are lazy – they just like trends, even when there aren't any. And there is no connection between Scottish bands, apart from the fact they're Scottish'.

Botramaid

Mid '90s A5 zine rune by Gail and Lorraine Douglas with interviews with the likes of Lunachicks, and fanzine and demo reviews.

Boys About Town

Focussed on all things Paul Weller, but produced in north of the border.

Can't Stand Limited Edition Records

From Ayr around 1980. Issue 3 had features on Positive Noise, Magazine, Monochrome Set and Bauhaus.

Charity Shopper

A Nineties zine produced by drummer Katrina Dixon of Edinburgh band Policecat. She subsequently performed and recorded with Sally Skull and later Tender Trap

Chicken Shit

Punk zine created by future Pastel, Brian Superstar & pals. Definitely of dubious value...

Coca-Cola Cowboy

Produced by Mike Smith and Paul Henderson from Glasgow & Ewan Mathieson of Edinburgh. Issue 1 had a great cover, and Issue 2 had a silly interview with the TV Personalities. The first zine to interview the seminal Boy Hairdressers. I'm not sure if these guys had anything to do with the Splash 1 club in Glasgow, but there are some similarities in the look and layout of this zine and the club flyers.

Coin Operated Press

Set up in the last decade, and based in Edinburgh, COP put call-outs for work, and produce collaborative zines from those submissions. Each callout runs for 3 weeks, Chloe at COP takes about a week to work on the zine, and then it goes off to print and is published shortly after... so, the zines are mostly published monthly. They are also involved with organizing Zine Fairs on the east of Scotland.

Cranked Up

Dundee music fanzine, *Cranked Up*, wasn't the city's first fanzine, with the likes of *Men from Soya* and *Le Sinistre* being very short-lived attempts earlier. *Cranked Up*, however, kept it going for 18 issues, so they had a very good run.

Crash Bang

A punk zine from 1977 created by a crew from Airdrie. This zine is mainly handwritten and looks a bit of a mess quite frankly. It puts me in mind of

Frances McKee's comment '.........I think I was thinking of making a zine that was easy to read for me, but Eugene and I were far too lazy to see that idea through....I couldn't be bothered reading most of them..the small type, the weird layout.....'

It features Scottish punk bands like Johnnie (sic) and the Self Abusers (soon to become Simple Minds), The Jolt and The Exile.

Cripes!

Cripes! was Bruce's Record's newsletter. Bruce's being Scotland's best known independent record shop chain during the 1970s. However, as a result of its association with the chain of shops, it became to be seen as a fanzine in its own right, and ran for two and a half years.

Edited from the Bruce's Edinburgh shop, *Cripes!* was put together by owner Bruce Findlay and Brian Hogg of the hugely influential 'zine *Bam Balam*, along with a number of other Bruce's employees. Brian reviewed Simple Minds several times, and suggested that Bruce should go and see them. Subsequently, Bruce became their manager, and signing them to his Zoom label, which had successfully secured a licensing deal with Arista.

It was included in the 'Oh So Pretty : Punk in Print 1976-80' book published by Phaidon.

Cult

An early '80s punk zine which was from Livingston.

Cute Kids on Medication

Dundee based zine. Issue 1 in 1992 has features on PJ Harvey, Rain Parade & Luscious Jackson. Don't know if there were any more issues.

Deadbeat

Deadbeat was an Edinburgh fanzine that existed from 1982 to 1986, edited by Vinny Bee, and ran for an impressive 33 Issues. Interviews with Strawberry Switchblade, Pastels, New Order, Big Country & Passionate Friends, amongst others. Vinny also branched out into releasing cassette tapes. (See more in C-30-C60-C-90 Go! Chapter). Also released a 7" single, 'About You' by Life Support in 1984.

Death on A Summer's Day

A collage in this anarcho-punk zine from January 1984 announces the fact that we had now reached the year depicted in George Orwell's dystopian novel. Some other zine reviews and music as well.

Disease

A punk zine from Paisley that was originally named *Torn To Threads* which had one issue published in November 1977. This was a 5 page/25 copy limited edition that morphed into the enticingly titled, *A Stagnant Pool Of Disease* before shortening the name for Issue 5.

Dogmeat

Straight outta Edinburgh in 1977. No other information existed which I could find about this zine, but I did wonder if it was named after the Flamin' Groovies song?

Easy Read

A zine produced by Dave Anderson from Kilwinning in 1997 and dedicated to The Trashcan Sinatras.

ENZK

A punk and hardcore zine started in 1989 by Graham Enzk, which ran for 10 issues. It was erratic in its output, with often several years between some issues. Issue 10 had a compilation CD of Scottish hardcore bands free with it.

Fagends

This may have been the one and only issue of this zine, which was edited by one, Glenda from Glasgow in 1980. I'd have been intrigued to find out more about this zine, as it is the earliest from Scotland with a female editor, as far as I can see.

Falling and Laughing

Started in 1983 and from Dundee with cassette label reviews and interviews with the likes of The Fall, M*rri**ey, Marc Riley, Prefab Sprout & Fanzine Reviews. Lasted at least 5 issues

Fast Product

Not a fanzine, but one of the first post punk independent record labels, set up by Hilary Morrison and Bob last in Edinburgh. Included here because they release two discursive fanzine interactions FAST 3 – *The Quality of Life* and FAST 6 – *SeXex*. Very influential on subsequent labels, not just in Scotland but UK wide too. Factory Records being a case in point.

Ferocious Apache

From Paisley. Issue 3 had features on The Redskins & Jasmine Minks. Very possibly edited by Andrew Burnett of Close Lobsters fame!

Firm'N'Fruity

Edited by future journalist and writer, David Keenan in the mid to late '80s. Featured interviews with The Pastels, The Vaselines, The Shop Assistants etc.

Fluid

Female edited zine from Penicuik. Not much info, apart from Issue 3 came out in 1996, and carried features on Delgados & Tunic

For Adolfs Ony

A title to be taken with a pinch of salt. This was a one off fanzine produced in 1977. Named after the single 'For Adolphs Only' by the Auld Reekie pub-punkers The Valves.

Fudge

Fanzine based in Aberdeen which came with a free CD of local acts. Was active in the early 2000's, but no idea if it is still going.

Full Moon

Another of Fritz Van Helsing's fanzines

Fumes

Late '70s and early '80s zine, based in Glasgow. Apparently the inspiration for young Robert Hodgens (aka Bobby Bluebell) to start his own *Ten Commandments* zine. Aztec Camera first appeared on a Glasgow cassette-only compilation of local unsigned bands on the Pungent Records label, given away with the zine which was run by Danny Easson, Patrick McGlinchey and John Gilhooly, who championed several Glasgow bands before they hit the big time. Featured the long forgotten Newspeak, which featured a certain Andrew Innes and Alan McGhee in its line up.

Funky Spunk

A zine produced by Manda Rin from bis, with stuff on hip-hop as reviewed by us in *Hype!* 'Amanda at FS obviously appreciates that there is more to life than indie'. Manda still agrees. 'We were definitely big indie fans but that term is also a broad genre where it can also dip into dance, electronic, hip-hop and ska amongst many others. Bis were/are a difficult band to describe musically and I quite liked that! I would always try to push the boundaries and discover bands like Luscious Jackson or Portishead who were out of my usual comfort zone. There's so much out there, it's just letting people know that it is'.

Granite City

Aberdeen based zine which had an interesting slant, looking at rock music's influences on comic strips. Covered various North East bands like The Tools. If it's the same Tools, they were from Alness and had an eponymous song with the immortal line, 'Alness/Such a mess/ You try so hard to be success/Full.' Superb!

GroundLeft

A zine about the hardcore scene, edited from Glasgow by Kirsty Dalziel in the Nineties.

Guilty of What

A 1980's Anarcho zine run by Spike in Stirling. Very Crass influenced. Spike seems to have become something of a guru on the subject in subsequent years. He was the drummer for anarcho bands The Apostles, Oi Polloi, Political Asylum and Part 1. He also worked with Optimo Record's JD Twitch in compiling the 'Cease & Resist – Sonic Subversion & Anarcho Punk In The UK 1979-86' – Double LP in 2023

Hanging Around

Started by Ronnie Gurr in 1977. Gurr later freelanced for Trax and NME whilst at Edinburgh Uni, before joining Record Mirror in 1979. An early champion of Scottish punk bands like Johnny & The Self Abusers.

Hard Copy

Eighties zine from Dundee. At least one issue was produced.

Heavy Flow

Edited by Saskia Holling who was the bass player in Edinburgh grrrl garage band Sally Skull around 1994, and still active in The Nettelles. This was another riot grrrl influenced zine about music and feminism. Using humor, irony, and sarcasm in this way was a typical marker of third wave feminism in the 1990s. She wrote a book Girlsville: The Story of The Delmonas and Thee Headcoatees which was published in 2021.

Here Comes Everybody.

Another Dundee zine which started up around 1981/2

Hiroshima, Yeah!

A current zine, which has been running for a long time now. Each issue comprises a few A4 pages full of poetry, reviews, short stories and diaries, assembled in a properly punk cut-and-paste manner, photocopied, stapled in the top left hand corner and posted to an unknown number of subscribers. Hard copy only, no internet presence. Put together by Mark Ritchie. For the 100th (!) Issue Mark put together a CD-r compilation featuring tracks by HY! readers, contributors and favourites

NME

ONE SMALL STEP (for mankind)

ONE GIANT LEAP.
fakes don't go disco!

issue four
Smalltalk
the dragsters · nikki sudden
jasmine minks · the pastels
blow-up · david westlake
ON SALE IN RHYTHMIC

THE NeW, IMprOvEd(?) 5TH

NEXT BIG THING

DeceMber 77
25p

in This iSSue...
RaMoNEs...TubES
BLue OySter Cult
ReZILLOS...ClasH
PiSToLS...

Plus
LoCal and
not so LoCal
nooz,
BLethers
and
Reviews

ARTOO, WHAT'S A REZILLO?

IF YOU'RE INTERESTED THERE ARE RAMONES, DAMNED 'N' BOOMTOWN RATS COMPETITIONS PLUS ...

DICTATORS Exclusive
HANDSOME DICK MANITOBA

SKIPPING!
< Kitten. >
15 newpence

'and also the trees'
Lloyd Cole & The Commotions
ASSOCIATES
N·M·A
...before the...
...suburban Area...
SCOTTISH ZINES
PIGSWILL
The Jesus and Mary chain
+ VERY WEE ON:

simpl thrild

YOUTH on tHE LOOSE!

WITH

Shop Assistants

That Petrol EMOTION

CLOSE LOBSTERS

AGE OF CHANCE

the soup dragons

& BMX BANDITS

THE JUNE BRIDES

also

THE HOUSEMARTINS

ALL THIS & MORE!

ONLY 30p

THE BEAT GOES ON

20 FIRST-EVER ISSUE

FAY FIFE WRITES HER OWN COLUMN INSIDE!
WILLIAM MYSTERIOUS — PAST, PRESENT + FUTURE.

FAY/EUGENE INTERVIE
REZILLOS ON WHISTLE TEST.

+ MUCH MORE INSIDE

ACME

RED HEADS,,,BUZZCOCKS..
R CUTLER... EUROVISION...
ONHEAD... |||||||||||||||||

TRASH'77

NUMBER ONE   APRIL 1977   ONLY 25P

THE SUB-HUMANS

THE DAMNED
LIVE IN
GLASGOW

REVIEW

THE
CLASH
999

HEY OLD HIPPY, YOUR DREAM'S
COME TRUE
WE ARE YOUR BLOODY REVOLUTION

pastelism

ISSUES 1, 2, AND 3

LEE HAZLEWOOD

DANIEL JOHNSTON

TEENAGE FANCLUB

ORANGE JUICE

"A" side

50P

SCREAMING
PuNk PLaNet

AN A-Z ALMANAC

£1

Positive
REACTION

POSTERS
GIG GUIDE
MUSIC REVIEWS
MOANY ARTICLES
GIRLS ROCK SCHOOL INTERVIEW

Issue #4
1st Run
46 /100

SLOW-DAZZLE

THE TV PERSONALITIES

Marc Riley & The Creepers

Miles Davis

SCOOTERS

ZAPPA

No. 4

PLUS...
PAPER SNIVELLERS, NAGMANN,
STIN SEX GANG CHILDREN, THE SMITHS,
TOMMY SWAN, THE LOVES EATERS,
GLASTONBURY FESTIVAL,
THE PASTELS

Pete Shelley

30P

Honey At The Core

Fanzine produced in 1986 by future journalist John Williamson, with a free cassette of the same name. As an antidote to the 'C86' bands, this one featured mainly Glasgow based future 'white soul' hitmakers such as Wet Wet Wet, Deacon Blue, Hue & Cry and The Big Dish. It's interesting to note, that, at the time of publication, more than half of the acts featured had no record or publishing deal, so it's clear this was an important stepping-stone in the careers of many. It sold rather a lot of copies.

Hungry Beat

A series of mini-zines by Jordi Maxwell featuring the bands from the post-punk scene documented in the eponymous book. 'I was asked to do the series by Douglas MacIntyre and Grant McPhee for a few events. I had done all my own research for it but had interviewed some of the musicians involved for my own interview series, *Fan De Toi!*'

Hungry Beat

Another semi-mythical zine which of which I have been unable to find out any info at all. May have existed in the 1980s and given its name to a book, but this is mere conjecture.

Hype!

Ironically named zine (actually named after DJ Hype of drum'n'bass fame). From the pen of this writer, with much assistance from Andy G, who wrote the 'Mad Crofter DJ' comic strip. Based in Inverness, ran for 3 issues during 1994 and 1995. Mainly covering the club scene in the Highlands, it also ran interviews with hardy indie perennials like Alan Horne (Postcard Records) Mark E Smith and Duglas Stewart (BMX Bandits). Included a free cassette with each issue featuring the likes of Bis, Inspiral Carpets, Trash Can Sinatras, Glory Strummers and the Hype DJ Collective. Formed Solar Records for limited edition Intelligent Tekno cassette compilation (1996 – 8 tracks)

Inner Space

A Tekno zine run by Chris Grafik from Edinburgh in the mid-1990s. Content expanded to include some artists promoted via London including Billy Nasty and K-Alexi. Regular features such as Hewligan's Rant, hand-drawn comic art and the editor's info and column remained. A well-stocked review section suggests that small labels, and bigger labels looking for kudos, were happy to be associated with the zine.

Inside out

From Edinburgh, 1978. Issue 2 was an Adam & The Antz special for the princely sum of 30p, whilst Issue 3 featured Scottish bands, Another Pretty Face and Flowers. It seemed to straddle both the late '70s and the early '80s. On account of its forward look, interviewing Hilary Morrison's post-punk outfit, Flowers, there's a proto-feminist element to it.

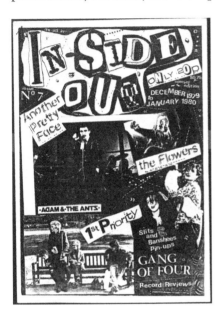

It Ain't Necessarily So

Scribed in 'skool daze' text by the future editor of *Joy! Joy! Joy!*. As he states in his second zine, he sold 60 copies and 'chucked it'.

It Ticked and Exploded

A 1978/79 – Renfrewshire zine created by Robin Gibson, a schoolboy from Johnstone, who would go on to become deputy-editor of UK music weekly, *Sounds*.

Ivor The Anarchist

Ivor The Anarchist cartoons had appeared in various fanzines in the mid-1980s and were created by John Green (script) and Mick Bladder (art) from Edinburgh. The first issue of *Ivor The Anarchist*, a funny and well drawn zine, and at 10p was definitely excellent value for money. It brings together several comic strips, featuring Ivor as a hopeless wannabe musician, and his band - the excellently monikered - Vomit Encrusted Chip Butties. Ivor was briefly resurrected later in the decade (See *Beyond The Gutter*).

JCHC Zine

A hardcore punk zine from Dundee. Put together the two compilations 'This Is Scotland not LA', in 2005 and 2022.

Jelly Bean Machine

'Brought to you from Glasgow for a mere 50p', courtesy of Claire. Issue 1 from 1995 has interviews with bis and the Yummy Fur. Don't know how long this zine ran for

Jingles The Creep

An excellently presented zine from the unlikely location of Camustianavaig on the Isle of Skye. Created by two brothers, Andy and Simon Goddard, who were still at high school at time of Issue 1 in 1986. Interviews with Brix E Smith of The Fall, Close Lobsters, Shop Assistants and more. With 3 issues in total, the lads branched out into the cassette world with the likes of their 'Dougie Donelly's Robot Pants' compilation on their own Yes, Mother Superior label.

Jockrock

An online website which, unusually, evolved into a printed zine for 4 issues. The brainchild of Stuart McHugh, who went on to run Is This Music? Magazine and Website. Interviews with Long Fin Killie, Spare Snare and De Rosa, amongst others

Joy! Joy! Joy!

From the Eighties. The editorial announces itself as 'the most inspirational fanzine ever to hit the streets of Greenock'. And who am I to argue?

Juicy Fanzine

From East Kilbride and published in 1997 – No Doubt, Lunachicks, Veruca Salt were all featured.

Jungleland

Set up by Mike Scott of Waterboys fame when he was living in Ayr in 1977. The first four were done in that location before he relocated back to Edinburgh, and ran the fanzine until 1979. Ran interviews with The Clash, Richard Hell, The Only Ones, Tom Robinson & Boomtown Rats. Always displayed an unhealthy Patti Smith obsession, reflected in the verbose output of his later band, the Waterboys.

Juniper Beri-Beri

Mostly written by Aggi (Annabel Wright) and Stephen from the Pastels with input from Jill Bryson. Their best quote has to be 'If you prefer your food straight off your girlfriend's stomach rather than on a plate, then the Vaselines are probably the group you've been waiting for,' when describing Kurt Cobain's fave band, The Vaselines. Nice cover designs by Aggi, and cited by many on the music scene as a favourite.

Jute City Hardcore

New Millenium Punk and Hardcore zine fae Dundee

Kingdom Come

Kingdom Come was founded in 1977 by Johnny Waller in Dunfermline, who published a new issue every few weeks for the next two years, before relocating to London. The first issue of this zine retailed at 15p.

Issue 2 billed itself as the 'local issue', and feature Edinburgh's Rezillos and Dunfermline's Skids

Johnny became manager to an Edinburgh band Visitors & owner of a short-lived independent record label Deep Cuts also based in Edinburgh. Two 7" singles were released on the label - Visitors: Electric Heat EP and The Fakes' Production - both in 1979). Both excellent by the way, and I think they're available on the Big Gold Dreams box set on Cherry Red.

After moving down south Johnny became a music journalist and also co-founded Fire Records with Clive Solomon in 1985. Sadly, he died after being hit by a car while cycling in 1996.

Kitten Frenzy

Ran to six issues from around 1994. Colourful A5 covers with features on iconic female performers such a Sonic Youth's Kim Gordon, plus gig reviews, travel and philosophy. Run by Glasgow band Urusei Yatsura. On the formation of the zine, Guitarist Graham Kemp has this to say, 'It started in 1989 in the queue for Sonic Youth signing the Daydream Nation album in RAT Records. I got an issue out in 1990, then started putting it out more regularly 2 years later once I roped in a few friends'.

Kung Fu Katz

Zine from 1999. Featured stuff on skateboarding, personal views, music reviews, zine reviews, clubs, shops, politics (interview with Tommy Sheridan – remember him?).

Last Hints

This zine was produced by the Clydeside Anarchists in 1982, and ironically subtitled 'The Magazine For Real Men'. The front cover illustration was based on Edvard Munch's 'The Scream', and draws out this theme throughout the zine.

The musical content consists of tongue in cheek articles about The Monochrome Set, the ultra-obscure Burma Blur (who I've never heard of) and John White who grew up near Sheffield and started his one-man project "UV Pop" in the early 80's.... 'their sound was regionally bleak and they used staccato, angular guitars lines, with vocals ranged from spoken repeated mantras to whispered and shouted political poetics'.

Le Sinistre

A precursor to the longer lived *Cranked Up* from Dundee. The name was taken from a Eurythmics b-side apparently. Lasted 2 issues in June and July 1981.

Le Tigre

A Riot Grrrl zine produced by artist Heather Middleton in 2001, and features Le Tigre (obviously) and other music and feminist articles.

Limited Conspiracy

Richard 'Jock' Watson started his *Limited Conspiracy* in Linwood in the early 80s at the tender age of 16 or 17

Kirk Brandon from The Pack/Theatre of Hate had a newly formed band called Spear of Destiny with a new LP and sound, and Richard interviewed him for Issue 4. There's also poem articulating the beauty of fanzines by Nancy Breslow, who was in fact one of the co-editors of US zine *Short Newz*.

Loop

Loop's playlist included The Shamen, Dead Kennedys, Electro Hippies & The House of Love. Issue 2 came with a free flexi by a band called Safe Houses.

Muzzle

From 1997 and produced by Mhairi McClymont and two school friends from Johnstone with two aims. Firstly, to get into gigs for free, and secondly to document the nascent nu-metal scene. Both worked, incidentally.

Next Monday's Exciting

Next Monday's Exciting is one of several zines that ripped off the NME logo, another being *New Musical Excess*. This was from the Stirling area, and came out at the tail end of the '70s.

Contains an interview with the editor of *Kingdom Come* fanzine about The Fakes from Stirling – an excellent rackety post-punk combo featured on the Big Gold Dreams compilation from Cherry Red Records with their track 'Sylvia Clarke' taken from the 'Production' E.P. As an aside, the titles of tracks B2 & B3 were not indicated on cover or label. The fanzine *Safe as Milk*, Issue 4, was the only zine to review the record as a four-track E.P.

Megazine

Run by Brian Speedie, John, and William from Stirling in the early '80s. 'The third issue contains an interview with Marc Bolan that was carried out in the 70s in Dundee by a friend of theirs. 'I think enough time has passed to reveal that I was the magazine's astrologer - Starboy - whose detailed predictions occasionally unsettled some of our readers', reveals Brian mystically. That issue also had the legendary Scrotum Poles 'E.P' as a freebie. Sold about 200 copies per issue

Men From Soya

Elusive Dundee zine. Maybe the first from the punk/post punk era. Stretched to a single issue. Green paper with a line drawing. Nice.

Mighty Mouth

From the rock'n'roll centre of Carnoustic in Angus, this wee zine featured Sunset Gun (the band not the zine), The Banshees & The Daintees

Murder By Fanzine

A zine from the wilds of Ross-Shire circa 1983. A good name indeed, but contents have eluded me.

No, I'm A Veronica

Early 2000's zine. Another produced by Mhairi McClymont and friends. Mhairi was one of the writers behind *Muzzle*. It was spurred into being by the band At The Drive In, but became 'conscious' very quickly. Covered topics such as contraception, race & identity politics

No Variety

A short lived 1977 zine cooked up by Edwyn Collins and James Kirk, Nu-Sonics and future Orange Juice-ers. James wrote political pieces and Edwyn wrote a retrospective on the VU's third album.

Off The Road

A zine put together by Pat Laureate of Melody Dog and later Vesuvius Records with an accompanying cassette in 1996.

Oi Division

Self explanatory 1981 zine. Issue one had Features on The Partisans, Exploited and Notsensibles, and was ridiculously overpriced at 20p. Oi! Oi! Oi!

Other Glamour (And Non Sexist Nights)

A 1980 zine from Edinburgh with female editors. Produced with the specific admirable intent of reducing sexist behaviour of men at gigs, and promoting a code of conduct to create a better atmosphere at music events. Also featuring a small section with the bands Flowers and Delmontes from Edinburgh. Sent to Rock Against Sexism in London (scanned for me by Lucy Whitman – at that time called Lucy Toothpaste, editor of *Jolt* Zine and writer for *Temporary Hoarding*)

Paper Bullets

Yet another of the bis-based zines from the 1990s. This one was edited by guitarist Sci-Fi Steven.

Pastelism

No surprise that this was a Pastels zine, helmed by Stephen P. 'Learn to Swim with The Pastels', was one useful article. As almost everyone knows, all the members of the band were in the British Commonwealth swimming team in 1984*. Oh, and they helmed the First Teenage Fanclub interview with guitarist and singer, Norman Blake.

*OK, that that second bit's not actually true.

Plain Sailing

See *A Boring Fanzine*

Pleasantly Surprised

Billing itself as Scotland's first audiozine (see chapter C30-C60-C-90 GO!). Pleasantly Surprised was edited by Robert H King, and his pal Elliot Gould (to become manager of soul-poppers Wet Wet Wet), from Glasgow. Issue one featured Cocteau Twins, Billy MacKenzie, The Wake, Primal Scream and Sunset Gun. Went on for several issues, compiling lots of interesting bands, and selling lots of copies.

Ploppy Pants

A hardcore crusty punk zine – which sounds altogether horrible! However, it was a well put together zine from the unexpected location of Sabhal Mor Ostaig Gaelic college on the Isle of Skye. Issue 12 in 2010 came with a free flexi-disc by the superbly named, The Wankys. Editor Roddy now runs Our Future, a micro-record and cassette label and an associated zine which comes out occasionally. *Our Future* Vol 2 in 2020 featured a 7" with features tracks from Sexplosion, Thisclose, Final Bombs, Decade and Dead Zen Men.

Poets For Sale

Published in 2020 by the Optimo Music label with all proceeds going to Glasgow Foodbanks. Says main main Keith McIvor - 'OM has always been in love with all things DIY but it took a global pandemic and months of being cooped up at home for us to get around to publishing our own zine'! Sold out its two runs of 100 copies.

Postcard Records Fanzine

This postcard-size zine was published by Alan Horne's Postcard Records, 'the sound of young Scotland', in 1981 and is mainly devoted to the label's two most important bands. The zine's A-Side is all about Orange Juice and the B-Side features Josef K , as well as telling the story of the label itself. It works like a single - with two sides, one for each band depending on which way you read it. Lots of info and colour pics, and biogs about the bands.

The zine was put together by an American music junkie called Barb, who moved to the UK from LA in 1979 and ended up working for Postcard. It has a professional layout and includes excellent photos of both bands. Some lucky people who sent off for it received a copy that had been signed by various band members and others managed to get a free copy of Orange Juice's highly collectable "Felicity" flexi disc.

Pop Avalanche Zine –

A 'Cross Border' zine from 1987 edited between Peterborough & Edinburgh

One issue feature the usual arch-commentary you would come to expect from co-editor Bob Stanley and a supportive critique of contemporaneous zines - *The Legend* and *Trout Fishing In Leytonstone* – which are described as 'a load of old cobblers' and 'trivial, derivative and monotonous' respectively.

Pop Hamster

Female edited zine From Penicuik from the Nineties.

Popgirls

And another from 1990s bis-world! Featuring Sleater Kinney and The Donnas

Process

Another of those long-lost Dundee zines from the Eighties. Minimalist. Only lasted one issue.

Positive Reaction

Anti-fascist punk zine from Aberdeen. Not much info available on this, but Issue 4 came out in 2017 in an edition of 100, with features on Dropkick Murphys, Brody Dalle & Discharge.

Provoked

A punk zine from Glasgow which ran for about a decade up to 2005. 'A motivated name and a jagged look is half the battle in zine presentation and *Provoked* comes armed with both. This zine spits out in big blackmail letters it's a punk zine' according to the Punk Rocker Website

Pub-Like Image

Geddit? An Eighties crusty/hardcore zine with the likes of GBH & Discharge on the cover. Sounds delicious

Pulveriser

An early '90s death metal zine produced by Bill. That's probably all you need to know.

Purdey's Gusset

Created by Janet from Glasgow. Fashion, hair, make up, review: Stereolab, personal comics, children's TV programmes, Spit and a Half record comix and zine label, lists. As for the title? I know not why.

Pure Popcorn

Edited by one Sushil K Dade from his bedroom in Bearsden, near Glasgow, along with Paul Woods, & Stephen Donnelly. Sushil was of course, later to find fame and fortune as the bass player with the Soup Dragons, ending up on Top of the Pops in 1990. Gave away the Soupies flexi which led to them being signed and ending up on the NME's C-86 cassette. Pure Popcorn Issue 4 was the final one – 'after edition 4 the time seemed right to call it a day. We had interviewed or reviewed so many of our favourite bands (Wire, Go-Betweens, Microdisney) it seemed like a good time to put our creative energies into something else. In my case that was the Soup Dragons. Getting a Single of The Week in the NME is something we could never have imagined and it really opened up the doors in so many ways'.

Riot Witch

2020's Riot grrrl zine from Edinburgh

Ripped & Torn

(Only for Issues 1-4 1976/77)

Scotland's first Punk zine. Tony Drayton (AKA Tony D) was apparently inspired to create the first issue of Ripped & Torn after bumping into Mark Perry of *Sniffin' Glue* fanzine during a visit to London in October 1976. Early issues were put together by Tony, Skid Kid and Grant McNally. A few months later he moved south from Cumbernauld (a new town on the outskirts of Glasgow) and continued churning out regular issues of R&T for the next couple of years. *Ripped & Torn* announces itself on the cover as 'the first Scottish punk mag written by fans...for fans' and proclaims that 'This mag fights against the customary, the average, the dull'. It's now been bound together in book form, much like *Sniffin' Glue,* and original copies go for an arm and a leg online.

Rocket 88

Well produced free Glasgow zine from the 1980s, edited by Stuart Spence.

Rockin' Bones

Lindsay Hutton of *Next Big Thing* fame formed the Legion of the Cramped – The Cramps fanclub with Mo*ris*ey in 1980. In tandem with this he published the *Rockin' Bones* zine from his home in Grangemouth until the Cramps ran out of steam in 1983.

Runnin' Feart

Billed itself as 'Scotland's top punkzine'. Also a record label releasing the likes of Gin Goblins and Toxic Ephex. Looks like it ran from about 1999-2008.

Screaming Punk Planet

Dave Emmerson's current punk zine. Does what it says on the tin, and rounds up punk bands and contacts from around the planet. Keepin' the flame alive!

Simply Thrilled

A 7" sized zine with a great free flexi featuring the Bachelor Pad and Baby Lemonade. Featured on the 'Big Gold Dream' compilation (Cherry Red 2019). Edited by Jim from Glasgow.

Skinhead Times

Who knew? A fanzine about skinheads and skinhead culture called *Skinhead Times*. Active during the early 90s, it ceased publication in 1995. Published by George Marshall, it aimed to remain non-partisan, and concentrate on music and fashion.

Skipping Kitten

Issue 2 came with a free flexi disc by The Shamen in May 1986. The two tracks were 'Stay in Bed' and 'Four Letter Girl'.

Slow Dazzle

Short-lived but very high quality zine, with interviews, reviews and features. Edited and published by Chris Davidson from Greenock. *Slow Dazzle*, contained some of the best writing about Scottish music of its era. Wide variety of music covered from Prince to The Pastels, and The Membranes to Miles Davis. Featured the first JAMC interview, although Stephen P feels that he may have got there first, with possibly the best cover of any zine in this book. Chris was very involved with putting on bands and club nights around Inverclyde, and still active to this day.

Small Talk

Greenock based zine. The writers were big fans of the TV Personalities. I also love it when a zine runs a feature, 'Whatever Happened To', on a band you didn't know had ever existed. So, what ever did happen to the Sherbet Tambourines? Answers on a postcard please.

Sniffin' Gravy

A free 8-page mini zine that came with Issue 5 of *Slow Dazzle*

Some Times

'Not Just Another Fanzine', claimed the editorial blurb on this Inverclyde based zine. I'm afraid that it kind of was.

Splish! Splash! Splosh!

Produced by Mark Ritchie from South Lanarkshire in 1988. Featured interviews with Soup Dragons, Shop Assistants, the Clouds, Talulah Gosh, the Sea Urchins, Remember Fun, the Groove Farm, the Rosehips, the Flatmates. Mark also produced a number of other zines, but struggles to remember dates, so I've included the listings here - *What Colour Are Your Pyjamas?*, *Sexual Fantasies of the Rich and Famous, Puppy Power and The Furry Terminal.* These came out in the late 1980s and throughout the '90s. Some of the interviews included Teenage Fanclub, the Wedding Present, Perspex Whiteout, Jad Fair, Daniel Johnston, Cornershop, East River Pipe, Tindersticks, BMX Bandits and Ivor Cutler.

S'Punk

Late '70s. From Dundee. Back in 1978 when Steve Grimmond and Craig Methven (of Scrotum Poles semi – fame) were still only in their mid teens, they started up this fanzine. So, we'll give them some leeway on the terrible name. At least thirteen issues exist.

Stand & Deliver

Started by John Dingwall and friends in 1980 in Glasgow. The zine regularly covered local bands and gave away the first recordings by Del Amitri and The Bluebells as a free flexi disc before they had official label releases. According to John, naughty highwayman Adam Ant nicked the title for one of his songs!

Strawberry Switchblade

A fanzine that never was, from the gang at Postcard Records. Important for two reasons. Firstly, it was intended as a vehicle to give away the first Orange Juice recording of 'Felicity', in the form of a flexi entitled 'I wish I was a Postcard'. These were included as a freebie with the band's first official release, 'Falling and Laughing', and spare copies given away with various zines such as Bobby Bluebell's *Ten Commandments* & *the Orange Juice* zine put together by superfan Barb. Secondly, the name was donated to friends of the band who were setting up their own all female combo. The rest is history.

Sunset Gun

Nothing to do with the Glasgow band of the same name, which comprised of sisters Louise and Deirdre Rutkowski.

This was zine produced in 1981 from Glasgow by Elliot Gould (see *Pleasantly Surprised*) masquerading as Klark Kent – and no that's not the Stewart Copeland from the Police's nom de plume! Possibly Superman though...

Also associated was the *Sunset Gun* audiozine (See C-30, C-60, C-90 Go!) which is advertised inside the zine. Its 1981 first issue had a decent track list –

A1 : H2O - Artificial Beauty
A2 : Sinister Turkeys - No Use (Crying Over Spilt Milk)
A3 : Final Program - Videophab
A4 : 30 Bob Suits - Life
A5 : Poems - Heaviest Action Wing
B1 : FK9 - Asking For It
B2 : Mao - The River Never Ends
B3 : Altered Images - Prayer Before Birth
B4 : Altered Images - The Legionaire
B5 : Orange Juice - The INtroduction

Sun Zoom Spark

A 1990s publication from Galashiels covering Alt-rock and Britpop bands. Edited by Brendan McAndrew from Borders band, Dawn of the Replicants

Sun Zoom Spark started off as a fanzine before relaunching as a colour monthly. The title was a Captain Beefheart track. Issue 6 from 1994, put Radiohead's Thom Yorke on the cover: 'I'm in a band ... I've got to be hard.' I knew it existed because I wrote some reviews for it............but there the trail ends. Although, apparently once it folded, it resurfaced for a while as *Trigger* zine

Surfin' Swordfish

This splendidly named Greenock based zine got 'Pick of the Week' in an unidentified magazine (Record Mirror perhaps?). Hurrah! Soup Dragons, Shop Assistants & The Loft were all included

Swankers

Alan Horne being naughty in the early pre-Postcard days................ aiming all manner of libel at his future flatmate, Brian Superstar, who was of course busy concocting all sorts on nasty nonsense in his *Chicken Shit* zine.

Sweet TV Times

Early '80s Dundee zine started up to promote the unfortunately named, The Junkies. Eek!

Texas Hotel Burning

A zine which came out in 1985. Issue 3 has a great cover. It was edited by Stephen Hunter from Stirling. Features a nice overview of Buzzcocks' recorded output, and recommends the 'Singles – Going Steady' compilation. 'Anybody with an interest in REAL pop history (Kinks, Bolan, Blondie etc) should have a Buzzcocks record or six in their collection'.

The Beat Goes On

A zine from 1979 dedicated to The Rezillos which came out until after the band had split up in 1978, strangely enough. Announces itself as 'First Ever Issue'. It may well also have been the last ever issue. Ironically of course, the Rezillos reformed and continue to tread the boards to this day.

The Bis(t) Wee Fanzine In The World.... Ever

From the pen of Amada MacKinnon (AKA Manda Rin), singer, keyboard player and all-round good egg, with said group, and one of several zines she produced. This was done in the late Nineties. And a very small zine it was too.

The Erotic Urges of Creeping Bent

Katy Lironi (Fizzbombs/ The Secret Goldfish) and Ann Donald (Fizzbombs/ Shop Assistants) put together a Creeping Bent zine that the label gave away, The *Erotic Urges of Creeping Bent* (BENT 014), along with some other limited run zines.

The Grass Is Green In The Fields For You

Matt Walkerdine of Good Press in Glasgow set up this 'small press investigating the unsung corners of music culture, its participants and visual culture' in 2019. Very much proselytizing the ethos of DIY and the anyone can do it approach. He also produces ephemera such as reprinting a Young Marble Giants zine as a flyer. Named after a Revolving Paint Dream lyric, as if you didn't already know....

The Incredible Shrinking Fanzine

A long running punk and metal zine from Edinburgh, run by Hibs book writer Andy MacVannan from 1988 until the 2000's. Featured bands like the UK Subs, Bolt Thrower & Naked Raygun

The Legacy

Inverclyde zine from the Eighties. Don't know too much else about it

The Next Big Thing

Lindsay Hutton started his long-running fanzine *The Next Big Thing* in April 1977. He took the name from the opening track of the first album by The Dictators - a proto-punk classic called "The Dictators Go Girl Crazy!" which was released in 1975. He took inspiration to get a zine going from closer to home – Edinburgh. 'Brian Hogg's *Bam Balam* and Bert Muirhead's *Hot Wacks* (where I first read Brian) were huge influences on me'. And from the USA '*Punk* was also a revelation as were *Back Door Man* and *Denim Delinquent*'.

The Ten Commandments

Influential indie zine run for four issues by Robert Hodgens, better known as Bobby Bluebell. The issue with iconic Orange Juice cover launched several careers including writer Kirsty MacNeil and photographer Robert Sharp, who both went to work for NME. Also featured free OJ flexi on an earlier issue.

The Voice

Follow up to *Cranked Up* in 1982. Lasted at least 3 issues

Those Times Bill Callahan Came to Fife and Hung Out in Scotland

A 52 page limited edition zine produced by Clare Archibald 2023, which blurs the real and imagined. Features members of Arab Strap and Mogwai

Total Beal

This punk zine came from Fraserburgh & featured the likes of Resistance '77 and Screaming Dead. Yikes!

Trash '77

Another zine featured in the 'Oh So Pretty : Punk in Print book'. This zine was put together by Craig Campbell from Glasgow with some help from pals. Issue 1 is an odd size and printed on shiny paper, almost like fax paper. They moved to a better print quality after this. Issue 3 has a split cover with The Clash and The Damned

Trigger

See *SunZoom Spark*

Tuna

Another Eighties zinc based around the Café Info Centre in Greenock. 'Fishwives tales and niggiling (sic) are something we don't need'.

TYCI

Glasgow 2013-2015. Free zine that covered feminism, art, film & music

Underfelt

......and another Geenock one. At 5p, you could have scraped about down the back of the settee and bought several copies.

Unskinny

A riot grrrl zine produced between 1993-96 by Lucy Sweet, who was Scottish reviewer for the Melody Maker in the early '90s. The zine was in comic book form, but wasn't really music based apart from a comic strip 'about a hopeless band called The Craps, who 'as far as I can remember were all called Steve'. Thanks Lucy!

Violet

A Nineties zine produced by artist Lucy MacKenzie, previously of the bands Batfink and Ganger. Aggi from the Pastels called it a 'really good riot grrrl fanzine'.

Visions

Dave Emmerson again. Skewed visions of beauty & some punk record reviews

Voices

Why do all these Greenock based zines from the '80s have titles starting with the last few letters of the alphabet? Did they all get together one day and decide, 'let's not call our zines ABC'. Anyway, this was an early one, from 1981.

Vomit

This zine was mentioned to me in 1996 by writer Duncan Maclean, so I'm unsure as to the veracity of it, but he reckoned that it was put together by editor/publisher Peter Kravitz in Edinburgh in the late '70s. Whatever the case, fanzines were a major source of inspiration for Duncan's *Clocktower Press*, which published early work by Irvine Welsh, Alan Warner & Co.

Waxbone Abdicate

Another Greenock based zine. Issue one had articles on The Smiths, The Fall, James and ZTT Records

What's It Like To Be Scottish

Who knows? Anyway, this obscure zine had features on The Groove Farm and The Wedding Present

White Stuff

Not sure if this counts as Scottish zine, although it was edited by Renfrew native Sandy Robertson in 1977. Sandy was a school pal of Alternative TV's Alex Fergusson. Headed for London after this and named his zine after a Patti Smith lyric in 'Ain't It Strange'. Robertson ended up getting a gig on Sounds newspaper, and going on to write books on rock'n'roll stuff.

Wrong Image

Another zine edited by Fritz Van Helsing from Edinburgh. One of the first zines to give write ups to Edinburgh post-punk bands Scars & TV21. During the Eighties he edited *Asylum* and *Full Moon* fanzines. Adopted the pen name Lou Kemia to publish this zine

Waxing Lyrical

An A5 zine from around 2000, with features on Ben Folds Five & The Supernaturals

X124

Produced after the demise of *Hype!* in 1995. More arts based than previous 'zine, with interviews with poet Edwin Morgan, writers Duncan MacLean and Kevin Wiliamson. Feature on record sleeve design with Chemikal Underground Records, bis, Urusei Yatsura & Spare Snare. Interview with Richard Hell following the publication of his first book. Duly massacred in the reviews section by, then unknown reviewer, Michel Faber. Featuring a silver heating insulation cover and a free Tunnocks Caramel Wafer. Cheers!

Bibliography & References :

Books

John Savage : England's Dreaming : Sex Pistols and Punk Rock – Faber & Faber, 1991

Simon Goddard : Simply Thrilled : The Preposterous Story of Postcard Records – Ebury Press, 2014

Simon Reynolds : Rip It Up And Start Again : Postpunk 1978-1984 – Faber & Faber, 2005

MacIntyre, MacPhee & Cooper : Hungry Beat – White Rabbit Books, 2022

Paul Gorman : Totally Wired – The Rise & Fall of the Music Press – Thames & Hudson, 2022

Neil Taylor : C-86 and all that: The Birth of Indie, 1983-86 – Verse Chorus Press, 2020

Various : Ripped Torn & Cut: Manchester University Press, 2018

Gavin Hogg & Hamish Ironside : We Peaked at Paper : An Oral History of British Zines – Boatwhistle Books, 2022

Nige Tassell : Whatever Happened to the C86 Kids? – Nine Eight Books, 2022

Loudon Temple : The Bungalow Bar : Been And Gone And Done It, 2021

Academic Papers :

Anderson, Robert (2015) Strength in numbers: a social history of Glasgow's popular music scene (1979-2009). PhD thesis: University of Glasgow

Maguire, Vicki (2010) Shamanarchy : The Life and Work of Jamie MacGregor Reid. Thesis for Doctor of Philosophy : John Moore's University, Liverpool

Taylor, I. (2014). From Analogue to Digital, From Pragmatism to Symbolism - The Cassette Tape as a Hybrid Artefact in Contemporary Popular Music. Paper presented at the Musical Materialities in the Digital Age, Sussex.

Ian D. Thatcher (2021) Introduction, Revolutionary Russia, 34:2, 157-160

155

Magazines :

Smash Hits, Sep 1980, These Intrinsic Intellectuals single review.

The Face, 1980 Interview with Rory Black by Ian Cranna.

The Quietus, March 2011, C86 And All That: The 25th Anniversary, Jim Keoghan. Roy Carr Interview.

Rolling Stone (Australia), December 1993, Interview with Robert Smith of The Cure.

Melody Maker, 1982, Profile on The Delmontes.

Quake, 1984, Interview with Robert Hodgens

NME, Oct 1978, Live review of Simple Minds by Ian Cranna.

The Times, July 1983, Echo & The Bunnymen review by Max Bell

Extract from article on 'Free Winged Eagle' in Scottish Magazines Network used with permission of author Josie Giles

Excerpts from Robert H King interview used by permission of the author which originally appeared in the Hinton catalogue, copyright Robert H King (Reprinted courtesy of Street Level Photoworks, Glasgow)

Excerpt from Lucy Toothpaste interview in The F-Word, 2011 courtesy of Cazz Blase

Film & Television

Big Gold Dream : The story of the Scottish indie labels Fast Product and Postcard Records 2015 – Reynolds, Simon : Interview

Information, Assistance, Fanzine Interviews
& Interviews for this Book

Thanks to the following for their invaluable help in some capacity – Lucy (Toothpaste) Whitman, Night School Records, Glasgow Zine Library, Glasgow Women's Library, John MacNeill, Andy MacVannan, Robert H King, Holly & Cazz at The F-Word, Street Level Photoworks Glasgow, Davy Henderson, Stuart McHugh, Sofka Zinovieff, Keg at the TV Personalities site, Colin Wilson, Kenny Stewart, Duglas T Stewart, Close Lobsters, The Delmontes, Mark E Smith, the band bis, Alan Horne, Janie Nicoll, Richard Hell, The Delgados, Urusei Yatsura, Margaret Chrystall for lots of local reviews and support, Michel Faber for writing for our zine and taping XTC for me, Terry 'Trance' Small for compiling the Solar Records cassette, Starsky for artwork, Julian Cope for the non-interview, Jim Gellatly at Northsound Radio, John Peel, Paula at Dedicated Records, MC Stoory, H-Ross, Stewart MacKinnon (Blam), Pete Light, Edwin Morgan, Kevin Williamson, Andy Goddard, Lindsay Hutton, Lucy Sweet, Jill Bryson, Brian Hogg, Rose McDowall, DJ MacLennan, David Keegan, Tony Drayton, Fay Fife, Stefan Kassel, Damien Love, Stephen (Pastel) McRobbie, Ross Sinclair, Saskia Holling, Douglas MacIntyre, Chris Davidson, Iain Morrison, John Dingwall, Martin Kielty, John Willliamson, Hamish Ironside, Ken McCluskey, Andrew Burnett, Gavin Hogg, Manda MacKinnon, Simon Hinkler, Les Pattinson, Mark Ritchie, Heather Middleton, Tom Worthington, Graham Kemp, Marc Masters, Dave Emmerson, Ruaridh Law, Lauren Thomson, Mhairi McLymont, Johnny Lynch, Jordan Maxwell, Michael Train, Keith McIvor aka JD Twitch, Ollie Pitt, Frances McKee, Joe McAlinden, Sushil Dade, Margarita Vasquez Ponte, Paloma Romero McLardy, Adam Sutherland and Highland Printmakers staff, Duncan MacLean, Hate Syndicate, Big Boy Tomato, Douglas Dreech, Johnny Moped, Bob Last, Steven Daly, Eddie Tudorpole, Tunnocks, Bernice Simpson, Brix Smith, Trash Can Sinatras, Inspiral Carpets, Spare Snare, Peter Easton at BBC Scotland, Glasgow University, Catherine MacPhee at Skye and Lochalsh Archive Centre, Josie Giles, Will Sargeant, Brian Speedie, Vinita Rocketgirl, Larelle Read, Matthew Worley, Scott Argo, Good Press (Glasgow), Simon Dell, Sukdhev Sandhu, Sci-Fi Steven, James King, Jan Burnett, Katy Lironi, Matt Walkerdine, Roger Hutchinson, Robert (Bobby Bluebell) Hodgens, Roque Ruiz.

Fanzine Covers & Artwork Material Courtesy of:

Douglas MacIntyre, Lindsay Hutton, Chris Davidson, John MacNeill, Michael Train, Graham Kemp, Simon Dell, Andrew Burnett, Saskia Holling, Dave Emmerson, Mark Ritchie, Heather Middleton, Iain Morrison, Andy MacVannan, Sushil Dade, Paloma Romero McLardy, Brian Hogg, Manda McKinnon, Lucy Whitman, Cherry Red Records.

All images in the book have been credited where possible. If there exists any error or omission within photo credits, please contact the publisher for corrections in subsequent editions.

Blogs used for background research:

For Malcontents Only
Still Unusual
Bored Teenagers
The New Vinyl Villian
Punk '77'
punkrocker.org.uk
Cloudberry Records Blog
Deadbeat Fanzine Blogspot
Rip It Up And Start Again:The Footnotes (Simon Reynolds Blog)

Podcast : The Fanzine Podcast with Bobby Bluebell & Alastair MacKay hosted by Tony Fletcher, 2023.

Special thanks and acknowledgements to Douglas MacIntyre for allowing me to use the James King quote from 'Hungry Beat', David at Earth Island Books for being so enthusiastic, and backing my ideas, Andy Goddard for proofreading a draft and gently directing me on things to leave out, and for discussions, gigs and pubs. Finally, Emma as always for support and encouragement. If I have inadvertently forgotten anybody, sincerest apologies.

About the author

Alastair MacDonald Jackson grew up on the Isle of Skye in the North West of Scotland, and developed a love of alternative sounds via the radio and cassette sharing in school. If he, or his friends wanted to buy records or tapes, it meant a six hour round trip to Inverness on the mainland, and that fact is partially what inspired him to write his first book for Earth Island – 'Dear Smash Hits, We're From Scotland!'

In 2010, he took up photography, and in 2019 had his first book, 'The Spirit of the Hebrides' published by St Andrew Press. It was longlisted for the Highland Book Prize that same year, and encouraged by this, Alastair continued his photographic journey, publishing a photozine with ADM Publishing in 2021. He then, over the course of two years, embarked on a travel odyssey - walking, photographing and camping on 42 west coast islands, with the best of these collected images being compiled in a book due for publication in March 2025 by Amberley Publishing.

He still lives on the west coast of Scotland, near the town of Largs, and is currently working on a photography project documenting Orkney and Shetland, which is due for completion in 2026.

https://www.alastairjacksonphotography.co.uk/

Ray wrote 'The Revolution Will [Be] Televised' because he fina[lly] realised that if our prese[nt] government wasn't going [to] trigger open rebellion, th[en] nothing would.

Instead, he has embraced [his] middle-class roots; where [he] used to be full of passion a[nd] rage, he is now full of artis[an] bread and locally sourc[ed] cheese. Meat may be murder [but] so are his knees. He's leaving [the] street fighting and stat[ue] tipping to the young. Inste[ad] 'The Revolution Will [Be] Televised' is an appeal [to] people from all backgrounds, to imagine and work for a better, fairer society with[out] the reliance on the straightjackets of traditional left-right politics or inherited privile[ge].

An important book in changing times, available now, direct from Earth Island Books, or any good book or record shop, or online retailer.

Remember, in this age of media, 'The Revolution Will Be Televised'.

EARTH ISLAND BOOKS

WWW.EARTHISLANDBOOKS.COM

ANARCHIST ATHEIST PUNK ROCK TEACHER

(A Memoir of Struggle, Grief, Philosophy and Hope)
By DaN McKee

Exploring the various ways in which anarchist philosophy, atheism, and a background in DIY punk rock influenced one conflicted teacher's approach to the classroom over twelve turbulent and thought-provoking years, 'Anarchist Atheist Punk Rock Teacher' is more than just a memoir of some teacher you've never met. It is philosophy of education, of anarchism, of authenticity, and of life. Throw in some personal history, the deaths of both of his parents to deal with on top of juggling all the professional absurdities that come with the job (not to mention having to teach through a global pandemic), and you have all the earmarks of a biographical classic.

Available now at
www.earthislandbooks.com

USED

ARTCORE
FANZINE
PRESENTS

NEFARIOUS

THE EVOLUTION AND ART OF THE PUNK ROCK, POST-PUNK, NEW WAVE,

33RPM   NA001

HARDCORE PUNK AND ALTERNATIVE ROCK COMPILATION RECORD

ARTISTS

1976 - 1989

WELLY ARTCORE

E EARTH
ISLAND
BOOKS

WWW.EARTHISLANDBOOKS.COM   WWW.ARTCOREFANZINE.CO.UK

Long before online streaming and even TV music videos, that were beyond the reach of many new bands outside of a lucky spin on the radio, the compilation became the most effective way to access, and be accessed by, the eager new ears and inquisitive minds of the then new punk generation. 'Nefarious Artists' is a field study of over 500 punk rock, post-punk, new wave, hardcore punk, and alternative rock compilations from their beginnings in 1976 as major label samplers and live showcases of the 'new wave'

HARDCORE HEART

dventures in a D.I.Y. scene

David is a 'lifer' - he's been around the block and earnt his stripes – and 'A Hardcore Heart' is not only a fascinating insight into the reality of touring with an underground hardcore band, but an invigorating time capsule of a punk scene before Instagram, Facebook and MySpace, even before mobile phones, sat navs and Google Maps. It's a veritable ode to being in the wrong place at the wrong time, an underdog story with (spoiler alert!) no happy ending, yet that won't stop its bittersweet narrative from putting a wry smile on your face.
Ian Glasper- Down For Life (and author of 'The Scene That Would Not Die' +)

Want to know what it was really like to submerge yourself in the nineties Hardcore scene? To live, eat, breathe, and be consumed by punk rock? Or what the reality of being in a touring band that lived hand to mouth and played more shows than the author cares to, or probably can remember, for the sheer joy of playing and not a whole lot else? Then you need to read 'A Hardcore Heart', a book that's a love letter to the intoxicating joy of music, the enduring power of friendship, loyalty, and the overwhelming desire to create something from nothing and forge a better tomorrow. Thoroughly recommended.
Tim Cundle – Mass Movement (and author of 'What Would Gary Gygax Do?'

Available now at

www.earthislandbooks.com

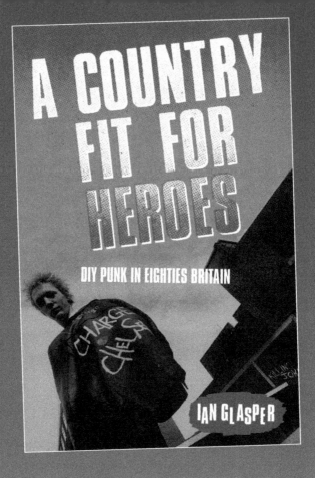

A COUNTRY FIT FOR HEROES
DIY PUNK IN EIGHTIES BRITAIN BY IAN GLASPE

Primarily collecting the stories of over 140 UK punk bands from the eighties who only released EPs and demos, or only appeared on compilation LPs, 'A Country Fit for Heroes DIY punk in eighties Britain' is a celebration of the obscure, a love letter to the UK's punk underground.

'A Country Fit For Heroes' plugs the gaps in Ian Glasper's first three books on UK punk in the eighties, performing a truly deep dive into that volatile subculture to create a more complete historical document of a most turbulent time.

With a foreword by Chris Berry, co-founder of No Future Records, this is an essential re for anyone with more than a passing interest in the UK's grass roots punk scene.

AVAILABLE NOW AT: WWW.EARTHISLANDBOOKS.COM

RUNNING AT THE EDGE OF THEIR WORLD : THE SUSPECT DEVICE FANZINE STORY BY TONY AND GAZ SUSPECT

The behind-the-scenes story of one of the U.K.'s longest running, and best loved punk fanzines. From the typewriter set, cut and paste layouts, to the illicit night-time, photocopying, up to today's comparatively slick output. The book is filled with stories right from the very beginning of the community they helped build and support, and still do. It's about the changes and challenges Tony and Gaz had to overcome, and the lifelong friendships created in the process.

This book is about the Suspect Device fanzine, but it's also about the punks who came together to create the scene based on the principles of DIY, friendship and co-operation.

You'll love it, and it may even inspire you.

As the foreword from Pete Zonked says, "Get off your ass and do something."

AVAILABLE NOW AT: WWW.EARTHISLANDBOOKS.COM

MY PUNK ROCK LIFE:
THE PHOTOGRAPHY
OF MARLA WATSON

MYPUNKROCKLIFE.COM
EARTHISLANDBOOKS.COM

The Scene That Would Not Die:

Twenty Years of Post-Millennial Punk In The UK

BOOK + CD DEAL

Available from:
www.earthislandbooks.com +
www.engineerrecords.com

AVAILABLE FROM EARTH ISLAND BOOKS:

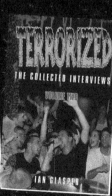

EARTH
ISLAND
BOOKS

WWW.EARTHISLANDBOOKS.COM

Milton Keynes UK
Ingram Content Group UK Ltd.
UKHW052023190824
447137UK00012B/152